Dear Reader,

We had the Year of the Woman. Now imagine the Year of You. One year, dedicated to you, to do with what you want. Okay, you can't actually take a year off—your boss and family wouldn't like that. But more and more women today are setting aside a special twelve months to get whatever they need most. You can do it—a year in which you say no to giving away parts of yourself. A year in which you say stop to the soul-eroding momentum of your life. You'll get a year where you . . . well, it's up to you what you get. A year of doing nothing, perhaps. A year where you make a small dream come true. Or resolve a long-simmering issue. Or learn how to play again. Or figure out where you want to go next with your life. Or do whatever you need to do. Let me show you exactly how, step by step, to pluck a year from the busy routine of your life and make it a year you'll always treasure. If you give yourself this special year, it can change your life.

—Mira Kirshenbaum

MIRA KIRSHENBAUM is an individual and family psychotherapist in private practice, and the clinical director of the Chestnut Hill Institute of Massachusetts. She is the bestselling author of four previous books, including *Too Good to Leave, Too Bad to Stay* and *Parent/Teen Breakthrough* (with Charles Foster), both available in Plume editions. She lives in Boston.

Let me introduce you to four women who did four different things with their special years. Their stories are just the beginning of understanding what's possible for you to get for yourself.

Abby—Figuring out what you want to do with the rest of your life

"I told everyone who makes claims on my time that I had some big decisions to make and that for a period they'd need to let me alone a little so that I could think about them. This was my year to slow things down in my life so that I could figure out where I wanted to go next.

"And in a little while I realized that I wanted to become a nurse. Ideally a midwife."

Jessie—Recharging your batteries

"Talk about running on empty. That was it. I had nothing left. I needed a year to do nothing. I had no plan, but I had a goal. Every day, I would do something special for me.

"If I wanted to wander down to the Y and swim for an hour, I'd do that. If I wanted to take a drawing class or yoga, I'd do that."

Nina—Having an adventure

"I didn't want my life to change, but I wanted some change in my life. I'd always dreamed of traveling right to the heart of Africa, the Congo or someplace like that—not as a tourist, either, but sort of living there with the people. So what if everyone said that I was a bad woman who left her family to go to Africa for a year. 'Hey, I'll come back, you'll get over it,' I said, 'and no one will get hurt. You'll forget, and I'll get something I'll never forget.' "

Kate—Finding a way to get on top of your life

"My gift to myself was a year to focus on doing my job without stress. All I wanted by the end was to be able to say to myself, 'Maybe you weren't perfect, maybe you weren't wonderful, but you were *cool*. To be honest, I felt scared and guilty going into my special year. Was I just being lazy and irresponsible? Here I get this big job and I focus on how I feel. It was the best decision I ever made."

THE GIFT
OF
A YEAR

*How to Give Yourself
the Most Meaningful,
Satisfying, and
Pleasurable Year
of Your Life*

MIRA
KIRSHENBAUM

A PLUME BOOK

PLUME
Published by the Penguin Group
Penguin Putnam Inc., 375 Hudson Street, New York, New York 10014, U.S.A.
Penguin Books Ltd, 27 Wrights Lane, London W8 5TZ, England
Penguin Books Australia Ltd, Ringwood, Victoria, Australia
Penguin Books Canada Ltd, 10 Alcorn Avenue, Toronto, Ontario, Canada M4V 3B2
Penguin Books (N.Z.) Ltd, 182–190 Wairau Road, Auckland 10, New Zealand

Penguin Books Ltd, Registered Offices: Harmondsworth, Middlesex, England

Published by Plume, a member of Penguin Putnam Inc.
Previously published in a Dutton edition.

First Plume Printing, April 2001
10 9 8 7 6 5 4 3 2 1

 REGISTERED TRADEMARK—MARCA REGISTRADA

The Library of Congress has catalogued the Dutton edition as follows:
Kirshenbaum, Mira.
    The gift of a year : how to achieve the most meaningful, satisfying, and pleasurable year
of your life / Mira Kirshenbaum.
        p.   cm.
    ISBN 0-525-94529-6 (hc.)
    ISBN 0-452-28214-4 (pbk.)
    1. Women—Conduct of life.   I. Title.
BJ1610.K565   2000
158'.082—dc21   99-042483

Printed in the United States of America
Original hardcover design by Eve L. Kirch

To every woman who dreams
of something better
for herself and her life

SPECIAL THANKS

First, I want to thank with all my heart a very special group of women. You know who you are. You are the women of brains and hope and courage who knew you needed to find a way to punch a hole in the cardboard box of your life. You had a dream to make come true. You had a problem to solve. You needed to find a way to take care of yourself. And you figured out how to do that in the middle of a busy, overcommitted life where you were sure you had no time.

It's not just for what you've done that I want to thank you. You are owed a tremendous debt of gratitude for sharing your lessons and stories with me and with women everywhere. Because of what you've done, new possibilities exist for all of us.

Next, I want to thank my partner, Dr. Charles Foster. This is our seventh book together. The simple truth is that we are full, fifty/fifty partners in every word of everything we write. Every sentence in this book is quite literally as much his as it is mine. And he's the love of my life.

It's a cliché that daughters can be critical of their mothers. Well, that cliché isn't true in my case, because I've received an incredible amount of encouragement and support from my daughters, Rachel and Hannah, during the long period when this book was hatching. I'm particularly grateful for their letting me know that the words I write make a difference to them in their lives.

The colleagues and friends I have to thank are too numerous to mention. They know who they are, and I've thanked them directly. Many trails had to be blazed to make this book possible, and I want to thank all my colleagues and friends for their various trailblazing efforts.

I want to thank my agent, Howard Morhaim, for his fine work and for believing in me through thick and thin. He's the best.

Lisa Johnson has been excellent in the important job of bringing my work to people's attention, and I'm very grateful to her.

It's terrific to be back with my brilliant and creative editor, Deb Brody. She really gets what I'm trying to do and, more important, knows how to make everything wonderful.

CONTENTS

"Dear Reader"   xv

The Basics

1. This Is a Year I'll Always Treasure
   "What is the gift of a year, and why is it important?"   3

2. On Your Mark, Get Ready, Get Set, GO
   "What are the basics for giving myself the gift of a year?" 18

3. Your Gift Should Feel Like a Gift
   *"Do I have to impress anyone with what I do in my
   special year?"*   23

4. The Secrets of Success
   *"Why should I feel confident I can give myself the gift of
   a year?"*   31

5. My Story
   "How did you come up with this idea?"   42

Discovering the Perfect Year for You

6. Paying Attention to the Real You
   *"What's a quick way to see what I need to do with my
   special year?"*   51

7. Find Your Acorn
   "What small shift will provide a major benefit in my life?"   58

8. The Ten Dream-Discovering Questions
   "How do I dig down to find what I really want in my heart?"   65

Considering New Possibilities

9. A World of Possibilities
   *"How can I see the full range of possibilities for my
   special year?"*   77

10. Just a Little R & R
    *"I need to recharge my batteries: how can I devote my special
    year to doing that?"*   86

11. Getting It All Together
    *"I've got to get on top of my life: how can I devote my special
    year to doing that?"*   93

12. Where's the Rest of Me?
    *"How can I devote my special year to exploring myself or
    putting the 'me' back in my life?"*   101

13. Beyond the Blue Horizon
    "How can I devote my special year to exploring the world?"   112

Translating Dreams into Deeds

14. Understanding and Accepting Your Needs
    *"How do I go from a vague to a specific sense of what
    I need?"*   123

15. You Can Get What You Want
    "How do I translate what I want into something I can get?"   129

16. Making the Impossible Possible
    *"No matter what I want, is there a gift of a year that will
    make me happy?"*   135

Giving Yourself Permission

17. One Thing Every Woman Wants
    *"Why should I feel absolutely 100 percent entitled to the gift
    of a year?"*   143

18. Yearning to Breathe Free
    *"Can I get a doctor's note that says I have to give myself the
    gift of a year?"*   152

19. False Solutions
    *"Aren't there other things I can do besides the gift of a year
    that will have the same effect on my well-being?"*   158

Making It Work for You

20. Getting Everyone on Board
    *"How do I get the support I need to make my special year
    happen?"*   167

21. The Wing Nut's Guide to Perfect Planning
    "How do I plan so my special year is a success?"   185

22. Finding Time
    "How do I get enough time every day to do my special year?"   199

23. The First Day
    "I think I understand everything, but how exactly do I start?" 210

Building on What You've Gotten

24. Loving Our Lives
    "How can I look for my special year to change my life?"   219

Dear Reader,

We had the Year of the Woman. Now imagine the Year of *You*. One year, dedicated to you, to do with what you want. Okay, you probably can't take a year *off*—your boss and family wouldn't like that. But more and more women are setting aside a special period to get what they need most.

At heart the gift of a year is just a little twelve-month stretch during which, in your own mind, you make yourself your number one priority. You devote one year out of your entire life to one woman—you. One year where *you get* the things you need, the things you really care about, the things you've been longing for. You claim some time for yourself and put some of *you* into that time. During it, you focus on what you need for yourself that will make this a year you'll treasure forever.

Whether you think of it as a treat or as a life saver, if you give yourself the gift of a year, it will change your life. If every woman in the world did this, it would change the history of women forever.

Before I began researching this book, I never thought there could be something like the gift of a year that would help so many women so easily and in so many different ways. That's why this book is a dream come true for me, and why I hope the gift of a year makes a dream of yours come true.

This is really three books in one.

♦ First it is a book that says, here's a wonderful gift that's made a lot of women happy. There are more possibilities for what you can do with your special year than you can imagine. So before you decide what you'll do with your year, read all the different stories of what different women have done, get some new ideas for yourself, and then have fun giving yourself your own gift of a year.

♦ This book will also show you *how* to give yourself the gift of a year piece by piece, step by step. This wouldn't be a true gift if at heart it weren't easy and natural. As one woman put it, "Nothing could be simpler. For one year you do something that makes you feel great about yourself and your life."

But if you'd like some guidance, you'll get everything you need here. If you need help seeing what you want to do with your special year, you'll get that. If you need help seeing why you're entitled to give yourself an entire year, you'll get that. And if you need help with practical issues, like how to find time or ensure you get everything you want from your year, you'll get that too. Oh, and don't worry if a set of recipes is not your idea of a good read. I feel the same way. Most of the practical help here is embedded in stories.

♦ Finally, this is a book about women and how we live our lives today. How we really feel about ourselves. How the way we live can drain the "you" from your life, and how important it is to take care of yourself and to fill your life with more of what truly matters to you.

I'd love to hear from you at Miraswomen@aol.com. Please share with me what you're doing with your year, what impact it's having on you, and any tips that will help others. The growing numbers of women who are giving themselves the gift of a year will thank you.

Yours,
Mira Kirshenbaum

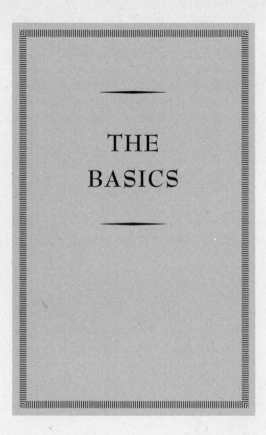

THE
BASICS

1

This Is a Year I'll Always Treasure

"What is the gift of a year, and why is it important?"

ou're a special kind of woman. You say *yes* to life and to people. You're responsible and caring, ambitious and hard-working. So you've piled your plate with commitments. But now your commitments have taken on a life of their own. They've taken over *your* life. Because of all the people you've said *yes* to, needs and dreams of your own have gotten choked out. What's best in you is suffocating, and you know it.

What's the last big thing you did just for yourself?

When a Little Is Not Enough

Sure, we all do little things for ourselves from time to time. You buy an outfit because you like it, not because you need it. You go off for a day with a friend just because the two of you want to reconnect. You say *no* to some outrageous unreasonable chickenshit assignment your boss gives you.

All this is good, but can you name something meaningful you've done just for you recently? You rearrange your life for others. When's the last time the people who are important to you rearranged their lives for you?

You work incredibly hard and make a lot of sacrifices to keep things running smoothly in many people's lives. Who works hard and makes sacrifices to keep things running smoothly in your life?

You can name a whole list of people who come before you in your life. Who puts you first? Do you ever put yourself first?

Not very often, I'll bet, and almost never in a really big way, in a way that really matters to you and delivers a big payoff to the needs and dreams and desires of your real self. I know . . . what else can you do? I *know*. My life is as full of commitments as anyone's. I'm married. I have two kids. I have at least two jobs. If I found a way to put myself first for once in my life and take care of what I needed to thrive—and I'll tell you how I did it later—so can you.

Whatever You Want

What *are* those needs and dreams that have fallen by the wayside for you? They're different for every woman, of course. With billions of women on the planet, there are billions of possibilities. Maybe what you need is to solve a particular problem—get on top of the stress at work, or find a way to get more fun and pleasure from your life, or stop getting involved with men who aren't good for you.

Maybe you want to make a specific dream come true—finally go back to school, or learn how to climb mountains, or take that trip to Paris.

Maybe you just need a real rest. Because sometimes simply doing nothing is the one thing your mind and body crave most. Or maybe you'd like to resolve a long-simmering issue in your life. Or get your life more organized. Or put the "you" back in your life. Or have some adventures. Or figure out where you want to go next with your life. Or do *whatever* you want.

Do you think you're the only woman in the world who's had to struggle with not getting her needs met? Of course not. Every woman struggles with this. And don't you think that with so many women in the same situation, an amazing solution would turn up? It has.

The Year of You

From women of all ages and backgrounds who'd heard about my work, I began hearing stories. These were women just like you and me. They too led busy, overcommitted lives. They too put most of their energy into doing what had to be done and into meeting other people's needs. But at some point the balance got too far out of whack. What about their own needs? What about their own dreams?

These women's stories were all about how they had dedicated a year to doing something special for themselves. That's *the gift of a year*.

Endless Possibilities

Every woman's special year is different. Listen to the voices of some women of different ages and backgrounds as they stand on the threshold of giving themselves the gift of a year, and listen to the very different kinds of years they're looking forward to. By the way, I happen to know that all these women pretty much got what they wanted. Why? For the simple reason that they spent a year focusing on it. They said, "This will be the year I . . ." and then they did it.

Susan. "I loved writing poetry when I was young. And it was good. But, you know, the weeds of everyday life kind of choked out any room for poetry. I kept saying, heck, you can always find a few minutes a day to do a little writing. But what happens is that you put out so much of yourself for work, family, and friends, that you're pooped. When you do have free time, all you want to do is tube out or zone out or hang out. The things that are really important to you that don't fit in to the boom, boom, boom of everyday life you just postpone. So I just said no more waiting for things to open up. They never will. No more saying I'm not going to do it unless I have all the time in the world. I'll never have all the room I'd like in my life for poetry. But screw it. I'm going to write a poem a week anyway. And I'm going to push things aside—big things and little things—

as I need to just to make sure I write that poem a week. This will be the year I look back on and say, 'I wrote fifty-two poems and saved myself from drowning.' "

Ann. "I've just been going, going, going. When have I been able to ever give myself the luxury of asking what I want to do with myself? You know what would make this year great? If I could just figure out what I want to get out of my life. Not what other people want me to want. Not what I think I should want. But what deep down *I* want in the sense that it's the truth of who I really am."

Julia. "I've been giving to others for so long. To say nothing of what my job's taken out of me. I need a year to lie fallow. I'm just drained. I know there's a minimum I've got to do, but beyond that I need a year to do nothing. I can't tell you how much I need a year where I do nothing but take naps, catch up on my reading—feed myself in all the different ways I've been hungry."

Ally. "I've been weak for too long. I mean I don't stand up to people, I go along with things I really don't want to go along with, I don't make things happen. I know there are strong women out there. I want to get some of what they've got, so I can be strong for myself. I want to take assertiveness classes and public speaking classes and martial arts classes and do everything I can to bring out the strong woman I know I have inside me."

Melissa. "I'm only twenty-nine, but still, I can't believe I've gotten to this point and I don't even know myself. I don't know what's wrong with me. I don't know why I do things. I don't know who I really am. What a great year this would be if I could just dig in and figure out what makes me tick. If I can just get a handle on my problems, I know I can start solving them."

Vicki. "My career's going okay, but for a long time I've wanted to travel to the Amazon to live with one of the native peoples. Don't ask—if you take anthropology in college, you get these kinds of ideas whatever else you do later. But I've diddled along and I haven't sunk my teeth into it. I know that if I focus on it, in one year I can make it happen, or at least get launched in it. I'm sick of postponing something I know will make me so happy."

Michelle. "I've been complaining about my job, my relationship, even where I'm living for a long time. The truth is I need to make a decision about them one way or the other, and I'm as far today from making those decisions as I've ever been. I'm tired of living up in the air. If I can make some final decisions this year, one way or the other, and end my ambivalence and get on with my life—this year will be a turning point for me."

Wendy. "I'm so sick of the way I've been phoning it in on my job. I'm better than this, and I can do better than I've been doing. I know I need to figure out why I haven't been so successful. If I can learn from that, this will be a great year. Then I can look back and say, 'This time you did well, you were successful, you came out on top, you made some money, you set a standard, and you met it.' I don't expect a lifetime of success in one year, but I want to do what I can to reorient myself toward success."

Do you catch a glimpse of the full range of possibilities, based on what women are doing with their special years?

The gift of a year is a time for you, and you can run around, if that's what you need, or you can stand still. You can do something different, or do what you've been doing in a different way. You can take something off your plate, or put something new on your plate. You can satisfy an old dream, or you can discover a new dream. Your special year can be anything you want it to be.

Don't be misled if I go on to talk occasionally about how one woman climbed a mountain, another woman painted landscapes, another laid the foundation for starting a business, another repaired her relationship with her father. You do enough for people already. The last thing you need is to worry about impressing people with whatever it is you do with your special year. Just take care of whatever is most important to you.

Above All, Enjoy Yourself

Whatever else it is, your special year should be a pleasure. Here's how Diana described what it was like for her.

Diana. "I couldn't quit my job, and I couldn't neglect my kids. But I realized I had to take my life in hand. I'd been feeling lost and unhappy, and I had this glimpse of what I wanted to do, which was somehow to reconnect to my love of nature. I'd always loved nature— biology and ecology were my favorite courses in college—but you know how it is. Once you're an adult you can get very far from things you really care about.

"So I guess I cleared the decks and found . . . well, I didn't find it, it was more like I stole an hour a day and a few hours on the week-end. And I just did things outdoors, bird watching, nature hikes, you name it. You know what I was doing? I was grabbing a chunk of time by the scruff of the neck and giving it to myself. For once in my life I'd have the year of me.

"I could just smell the way this year would be my year, the way you can smell a bakery around the corner. And I knew that I'd somehow help myself turn a corner by the end of it. It's funny be-cause I never thought I could afford it, time-wise, but sometimes if you just decide to do something, it's all there for you."

By reexperiencing her love of nature, Diana made an amazing psychological shift. Before her special year, her future had seemed foggy—lacking much of who she really was and what she cared about most. Afterward, she said the whole year she'd felt as though the sun had come out. Based on how pleasurable her year was, she now envisioned her future filled with wonderful experiences and real growth in her appreciation of the natural world. And all that from doing something that was so easy and so much fun for her.

Playing for Keeps

You might say, well, la-di-da, what a nice little luxury the gift of a year is. Just what the world needs: more self-indulgent women.

If I believed that I wouldn't have written this book. I was a poor kid, a refugee kid. Because my parents survived the Holocaust, when I was a little girl I sometimes imagined the Angel of Death standing at the foot of my bed asking me, "Why should you have lived when so many others died?" Survivor guilt. Lots of us have it. And it makes you take things seriously. So do you think I'd be busy with the gift of a year if it was just frosting on the cake? Okay, yes, for many women it tastes as sweet as frosting on a cake. And what's wrong with enjoying something wonderful?

But make no mistake. The gift of a year can in a way save your life. You need to think of your special year as an absolute necessity. Because it is.

Have you ever said something like, "It's time I did something just for me"? If you have, that's good. It's a sign that maybe something's going on that you need to pay attention to before it's too late. When carbon monoxide leaks into your house, you can suffocate before you realize what's happening. The same kind of thing happens to far too many women today. We pour our energy into what we have to do for others. Even if you're doing well at your chosen career, most of what sucks the time out of your life is duties you have not chosen. Meanwhile who you are, what you need, *what's best about you* gets deprived of air and slowly starts to suffocate.

Let's get real. What do you think will happen if you don't make yourself a priority in your life for one year? What do you think will happen to the dreams you need to make come true? To the parts of yourself you have to take care of? To the problems you have to solve?

Restoring the Natural Balance

Why do you think depression is a problem for five times as many women as men? All you need to know is that women are five times less likely to say *yes* to themselves than men. Isn't that a recipe for depression? After all, depression can happen to us when the self gets worn out and discouraged from our not doing a good job taking care of it.

How can you think of yourself as a caring person if you don't take care of yourself? If you don't take care of yourself, you'll stop thinking of yourself as someone who has a lot to give. Instead you'll feel deprived. And you'll hate your life. How can you give others joy if you can't give yourself joy?

Giving yourself the gift of a year has a magical impact on your life because it restores the natural, necessary balance between giving to yourself and giving to others. There's no reason for you to leave yourself outside of the equation. In the ecology of your life, you're as important as anyone. If things curdle inside of you because you've neglected yourself, then ultimately they curdle for everyone.

Instead imagine a small life-saving miracle. You give yourself a year in which you say *stop* to the soul-eroding momentum of your life. You give yourself a gift you've never given yourself before. Instead of putting yourself last, by hook or by crook *you do what you need to do for yourself.*

Maybe it only takes a few minutes a day. Or an hour a day. Or, for some women, a bigger chunk of time. But you give yourself one year that will stand out forever in your memory as a year different from all the others.

That's the *gift* part of the gift of a year. A real gift has to be something personal, something with impact, something you care about, something that gives you pleasure. So does your year.

Time Is on Your Side

What about the *year* part? Of course you realize that I'm talking about whatever time you can find and afford over the course of a year. I will talk about time a lot—it's a big issue for us overcommitted women. And I'll prove to you that you will be able to find the time to give yourself the gift of a year that's right for you. For now, one brief example. An hour a day for one year is 365 hours. That equals *more than nine entire work weeks.* What can't a woman accomplish in that time?

It doesn't even have to be one year. Gifts aren't rigid. But I know this—it can't be a day or a week. That doesn't even come close. We give ourselves a few days here and there all the time. But come on. A little is not enough.

The point of talking about a year is that it's big and memorable. It does something substantial for you. If you went on a religious retreat or took a trip you've dreamed of or went to an artists' colony for two solid months, leaving everyday life to do it, well, that's huge. That's two months full time, and anyone would say that's the equivalent of a year part time.

Your gift of a year can be more than a year too. If you want it, you might be like many women for whom the gift of a year turned into the gift of a lifetime. Why would you stop if it feels good and it's working for you?

The point of a year is to seize hold of a large enough chunk of your life so that even when you're an old lady that chunk stands out in your memory. The point of a year is also to make something of your own a priority long enough to really make a dent in it or resolve it or complete it.

So there's nothing sacred about the exact time span of 365 days. But feeling that you're worth something like a year—that is sacred.

The Rhythm of Your Life

Working within the rhythms of time—that too is sacred. Women have a special relationship with time. Menstruation, aging, birthdays, the biological clock, the ceremonies for which we feel responsible— all these give us an unusual awareness of time. Time as something to treasure, time as a resource, time as the arena in which we live our lives.

We focus too much on time as the enemy—aging, for example. On time as the scarcest of resources—our feeling incredibly busy, for example. But more than anything we're used to flowing with the river of time. Time isn't our enemy. It's our home.

This is where the gift of a year comes in. We talk about wanting to do something before a certain age or within a certain period of time. We understand how precious a year can be, and how powerful. You can make a baby in that time. So it's natural to give ourselves a year to do something special. When you give yourself the gift of a year, you know you're working with a time-centered process that for women is the most natural thing in the world.

You've Got All the Time You Need

Sometimes when I talk about the gift of a year a woman says, "But I'm just too busy." I sympathize, I understand. We're all going nuts these days. I am bruised by the same time crunch that squeezes in on all of us, but I'm telling you that *you can and will find time in your life to give yourself the gift of a year.*

You'll find plenty of material later in the nuts-and-bolts part of this book about how to get more time and support for yourself. But to prove that you can do it, let me just summarize:

WHY YOU *DO* HAVE TIME TO GIVE YOURSELF A SPECIAL YEAR

1. You'll be so excited once you discover what you want to do with your special year that you'll find time you didn't know you had.
2. Most of the things most women want to do with their special year don't take all that much time from their day or their week.
3. Yeah, you're busy, but nine out of ten women do have some free time for themselves, and I bet you do too. Just because we piss away too much of our free time doesn't mean we don't have it.
4. The problem is not that you can't find the time, it's that you haven't said *no* to the people who make demands on you. You don't have a time shortage, you have a saying-no-to-others shortage.

It's a reality that we're all busy. But it's time we stopped using "I'm too busy" as an excuse to deny ourselves what we desperately need.

You deserve it, damn it. Speaking of excuses, I'm sure you like to think of yourself as someone who has a lot to give. How do you square that with the gift of a year? With a world full of people who need what you have to give, how can you justify giving a special year to yourself?

Ah, there it is. The voice of doubt. The part of you that tries to talk yourself out of giving to yourself. This voice is real. Let's let it out for a moment. Every woman who's given herself a special year has heard the voice of doubt. Based on what women have told me, here are the top ten excuses they've come up with. Listen to all the insidious ways we deprive ourselves.

Top Ten Reasons *Not* to Give Yourself the Gift of a Year

1. "When your husband/boss/boyfriend/mother needs you, you've got to be there or else."
2. "There's always next year, or the year after, or when you retire."
3. "There's nothing you really want to do that you're not already doing."
4. "Once you start paying attention to what you care about, maybe you'll go crazy and go overboard and just want more and more for yourself."
5. "Truly moral women put themselves last on their list of priorities."
6. "What you really want is something you'll enjoy, and what does it say about you that you'd do something just because it makes you happy?"
7. "Your friends will hate you if you're not as miserable as they are."
8. "After all, women don't know what they want anyway."
9. "Maybe you'll discover something wonderful you want to do more with, and wouldn't that be inconvenient for everyone?"
10. "You're not really worth it, are you?"

You don't believe any of this crap, do you? Of course not. And yet, words like these make some women hesitate. Well, watch out. She who hesitates is lost. The fact that you need to give to yourself as well as to others is a lesson you can learn the hard way or the easy way. I hope you learn it the easy way. Here are two women who learned it the hard way.

Maggie's Story

"My sister Sarah saved my life. But I wasn't able to save her life. Not in any way. No matter how hard I tried.

"We grew up in one of those rust-belt towns of the Midwest that were slowly decaying back in the early eighties. On a quiet night you could stick your head out the window and hear the opportunities drying up. Most of the people we knew didn't have a lot to look forward to.

"Sarah was my older sister, and she just had a sense about things. She knew I was good in school and that if you had some education, you could do anything. I don't know what wise inner core she got this from, but she decided that I should be the one to go to college because that way at least one of us would have an easier life. She would talk to me about this. 'Look, Maggie,' she said, 'I'm just going to have some job anyway. But you've got a chance. You do well in school. You can be anything, a nurse, a teacher, anything. You let me help you, and when you're a success, that will be my reward.'

"I was too young then to argue with her. She'd always been my older sister who took care of me. I took for granted what Sarah was doing and saw how it made sense. But inside I told myself I'd repay her some day. Sarah would never let me talk about repaying her, but that's what I wanted to do. You always think there will be time.

"Now let's fast forward. Sarah was right. I did well in college, I went to law school, I moved to the East Coast. And none of it would've been possible without the money and encouragement my sister gave me.

"I never forgot about paying Sarah back. But how? Sarah wouldn't take any money from me. Even though she needed it. She led the life you lead when you're a waitress and your husband drives a delivery truck. And you have four kids. Your life just gets away from you. But she couldn't stop me from setting up a little fund—not that I had that much money myself—to help her kids eventually go to college.

"Sarah's life wasn't bad. But it had a hole in it where Sarah should've been. She ran around busy, doing for others, doing what had to be done, denying her dreams for herself.

"We talked on the phone all the time. Come on, Sarah, I'd say, there's got to be stuff you want to do for you. You always used to like to draw and you were so good at it. Maybe go back to school. Your kids are older now.

"But all she could see was the spiderweb of duties she'd woven around her. She would start listing her *gottas*. 'Look, Maggie,' she'd say, 'I've gotta this and I've gotta that and when that's done there's a bunch of other stuff I've gotta.' Then she came out with it. 'Maggie, stop asking me to think about myself,' she said. 'It just makes me feel bad, and there's nothing I can do about it.'

"Checkmate. What could I do? It was like she was saying let me drown. It made her unhappy to think about making herself happy. And the trump card she used to shut me up was that there would be this time in the future when she'd be out from under. Her kids would be gone. And she could do what she wanted.

"Then the roof fell in. Her oldest daughter, sixteen, got pregnant and decided to keep the baby. We could all see Sarah's days of taking care of people going on and on. God knows she was used to it. Proud of it. But you could tell it was a huge disappointment to her. And then she got sick.

" 'Maggie, my life is turning into a soap opera,' is how Sarah began the conversation where she told me the bad news. That she had uterine cancer, that it was pretty far along, and that it didn't look good.

"Everyone was there for her, including me of course. She didn't have to lift a finger. It turned out she didn't have a lot of time left, but she used her time well. I still have all the watercolors she finally got around to making during those last months. The first art she'd done in twenty years. All sunsets. 'Because I like the colors,' Sarah said, 'and I want to see if I can get them right.'

"When someone is sick the way Sarah was, you spend a long time saying goodbye. I still can't talk about our last conversation, but let me tell you about our next-to-last conversation. This was the one where Sarah still felt strong enough to be my big sister and pass on some last words of advice.

" 'Maggie, you turned out just the way I'd hoped. See, wasn't I right to make sure you gave yourself the kind of life you've gotten? But you know, you and I are the same. Duty comes first. And that's great. But maybe I steered you wrong. You know, you can work so hard you forget to have a life, and who you really are kind of gets lost in the shuffle.

" 'So I want you to promise me you'll take time for yourself somewhere along the line, a big chunk of time. Don't do what I did. Don't neglect what you care about, what you need.' Sarah leaned forward in bed. 'I think at the end we're all called to account for what we did for others. But we're also called to account for what we did for ourselves. Give yourself some time when you come first.'

"It was so painful hearing Sarah say that. What she was giving me was really a commentary on her own life. How typical of her to be brave enough to face her regrets at the very end but turn them into something I could use."

Don't Let Yourself Get Kidnapped

This story makes me cry, but it also makes me mad. Let's put Sarah in perspective. She wasn't a saint. A life of sacrifice wasn't the life she'd dreamed of. Sarah was no more and no less than a truly good person who was kidnapped into a life of duty. She deserved better. She deserved to find a way of being a person for herself instead of being defined only by what she did for others.

At the very end, Sarah gave herself something like the gift of a year by giving herself time to focus on her watercolors. *Finding something you care about and plugging it into your life—that's the key.*

I'm glad Sarah found something for herself before it was too late. But let's face it. At the end, she was not only eaten up with cancer, she was eaten up with regret, although she heroically tried to hide it. Make no mistake about it. Neither Sarah nor you nor I were designed by nature to run on empty. If you don't give to yourself, you will suffer damage.

Nourishing Yourself

Look, you're terrific because your strength and your character have caused you to pile your plate full of responsibilities. But you are the soil out of which your own life springs. To be fully and com-

pletely the best you can be, you have to feed that soil. You are capable of giving so much nourishment to others. You have to nourish
yourself. *That's* what the gift of a year is all about.

If your life goes on the way it's been, will you say you've done
what you need to do to take care of yourself?

Will you say you've gotten all you want from life?

Will you say you've truly tapped what's best in you?

Will you say you've given yourself all the rich and special memories you'd like to have?

Will you say you've gotten everything you deserve?

I've written this book because it must stop—the way you and I
have not found room for ourselves in our lives. When you make
yourself a top priority in your life for one year, you prove to yourself
forever that you're free, not trapped. You prove that you own your
life, instead of feeling that everyone else's claims on you come first.
You prove that you can take care of yourself. You change the way
you feel about your life forever.

So do it now: cut one big slice from the pie of life and give it to yourself.

2

On Your Mark, Get Ready, Get Set, GO

"What are the basics for giving myself the gift of a year?"

So how do you do it—go out and give yourself the gift of a year?

The basic program couldn't be easier. I learned it from women who've had the pleasure of waking up every morning looking forward to the next day of their special year. How could it be complicated if so many women doing so many different kinds of things found it simple?

Having such a simple program is important because it gives you flexibility. It's as if you were asked, "How do you eat breakfast cereal?" There are so many different cereals, and each of us has her own way of eating them. One person can't stand it if her corn flakes aren't crispy crunchy. Another loves to let her raisin bran sit in the milk because she says it makes the raisins plump and juicy. So you can't go into incredible detail with your instructions. You just say, "Pour some cereal in a bowl, add milk and maybe a little sugar or honey, maybe even some fruit, and just start eating," and then let individuals be guided by what makes them happy.

In the same way, when it comes to the gift of a year every woman is different from every other woman, and each of our lives is different. *The point is that the right way is the way that's right for you, as long as you do the basics.* Here are the basics that apply to everyone:

The Gift of a Year
THE BASIC PROGRAM

1. *What do you want?* Figure out what you really want to do with your special year and what you want to get out of it.
2. *Why do you deserve it?* Make sure you feel fully entitled to take a little time for yourself and say *no* to some people and obligations you've been saying *yes* to.
3. *How will you get it?* Know how you're going to fit whatever it is you want for yourself into your year and into your daily life.

The rest of this book is a ground-level stroll through the terrain you've just caught a bird's-eye glimpse of. By the end, you'll have everything necessary to get your specific needs met when it comes to your special year.

♦ Some women need help figuring out what they want to do with their special year. Are you one of them?

Maybe you need help digging right down to your core to identify from the inside what it is you really want. You'll get that. Or maybe you have a vague sense of what's missing, and what will really help most is seeing what's possible. You'll get that too. Once you see the amazing range of what other women have done with their gift of a year, *bang!* you'll see what you want to do.

♦ **Some women need help feeling fully entitled to take a little extra time for themselves. Are you one of them?**

The fact is, the biggest boost in your sense of feeling "I deserve this" comes from hooking up with what you want to do with your special year. Once you can almost taste it, you will feel entitled to it. But later you'll get specific help. Nothing gives you a stronger sense that you're entitled to a special year than the following.

1. You need to know whether you're suffering from a potentially serious condition I call *suffocation-of-the-self syndrome*. If you are—and you'll find that out—you will certainly feel all the permission you need to give yourself the gift of a year.
2. You need to know whether you've been dealing with your sense that your true needs aren't being met by using false solutions. You'll see what these false solutions are and whether you've been using them.

♦ **Some women need help getting clear about how they're going to fit what they want into their year or into their daily life. Are you one of them?**

When it comes to the practicalities, women have three main questions: *How will I find the time I need? How will I get support from the people who are important to me? How can I make sure that what I want to do fits into what's possible for me since I only have one year?* For each of these questions, you'll find the answers you're looking for.

Going through the basic program is like getting your dream house. I've never done this myself; I've been living in the same old house for quite a while now. But people tell me that, first, you sit down with an architect and you talk about *you*—how you live, what you need, what you want. Everything begins with your own desires. Do you entertain a lot? Do you like to wake up with the sun on your face? The details are endless, but soon your desires take shape.

Then you and the architect talk about all the possibilities. Perhaps to help you zero in on exactly what kind of house you'd like, she introduces you to new possibilities for windows and flooring and room design you haven't thought of. Often new possibilities stimu-late new desires. Or they help you discover your true desires.

Then you probably have a moment when you suddenly feel, "This is too much. I can't afford it." This is when you need what-ever will work to make you feel that you've paid your dues and now truly deserve your dream house. Fortunately, the gift of a year, un-like a dream house, is free!

Then what? There are always how-to details to get through. With a house you have to get financing; with a special year, you have to find time.

But let's step back and view the basic program as a whole. There's a message here. The program is saying: "Never forget: this is your year. It's got to be based on what you really want for yourself. This is the one time in your life when you need to focus on what matters to you, what's been missing for you, what will make you happy."

It's also saying: "You might think a lot of psychological issues are involved, but there's really only one transcendent issue. Do you truly feel entitled to a special year? Do you feel so much permission that it's as if God has commanded you to give this to yourself? You need this strong a sense of permission, or you might cave when peo-ple make demands on you. How will you stand up for yourself if you don't feel entitled to?"

And this program is saying: "Make sure you get what you need to make your special year happen. Don't be afraid to set things up so that your year will go smoothly."

On some level, could anything be easier? *How do you give yourself the gift of a year? You just have to know what you want, know why you deserve to get it, and know how you're going to get it.* It's like great sex. We might face our share of hurdles on the way to getting great sex, but it's awfully nice to know that in principle it's easy, because it's natural—you were designed by nature to get it.

Of course, different women need different things. A few women already have what they need. But most women have some ques-tions. That's why I wrote this book. I don't want anyone to feel embarrassed because she has hurdles to overcome. There are ways we all need help. Making cookies from scratch is easy too, but if you don't know that you have to have the butter at room temperature before you cream the butter with the sugar, you can get awfully frustrated.

While this program is simple and basic, it's also utterly revolutionary. As women we are still surrounded by voices that make us doubt whether we're entitled to base our lives on what we want for ourselves. This of course makes it hard for us to know what we want for ourselves. No wonder we sometimes run into trouble getting what we want.

The basic program for the gift of a year turns all this upside down by focusing first and foremost on what you need and want. That's why for many women it's been the first step into a new future, regardless of what they actually did for themselves during their special year.

I think we're all hungry to know there's a basic simplicity underlying the complexities we face, to know that beyond all the difficulties the answers we're looking for are basic and solid. Now you see that a basic simplicity lies at the heart of the gift of a year. Why should it be complicated to punch air holes in the box of your life to save what's best about you from suffocating? You can feel confident that what you have to do to give yourself the gift of a year is easy and natural.

3

Your Gift Should Feel Like a Gift

"Do I have to impress anyone with what I do in my special year?"

he most important thing to know is that the gift of a year should feel good. You should enjoy it. It should make your life better. It should feel easy. It should be a pleasure. Maybe you'll decide to do something strenuous with your special year. Maybe you'll decide to accomplish something important, or at least something deeply meaningful for you. Fine. That's your choice. If that's what you need to do to take care of yourself and get what's been missing in your life, that'll be great. *It's your special year.*

But the key is taking care of yourself. The key is getting your needs met. The key is feeling happy and healthy, centered and in control. Maybe you'll end up wanting to put a lot of effort into it, but for now, think about your special year as possibly being something completely effortless.

As Easy as Can Be

Let's meet two women who found that giving themselves the gift of a year was incredibly easy. I'll be honest with you—not every woman has such amazingly smooth going as Theresa and Amanda. But the stories of these two women certainly drive one point home: they show how simple the basics can be.

Theresa. For a while now Theresa had been filled with spiritual longing. The church had once meant something to her, but for seven years she hadn't set foot in a church. Now she wanted to reestablish that connection. The minute she heard about the gift of a year she knew what it would be for her. What she'd do is go to church every day, and what she'd get is a chance to radically jump-start a whole new relationship with God.

She'd go to services when they fit her schedule, and she'd go to sit and pray when she couldn't go to services. Theresa figured that a year of talking daily to God in church would be the most wonderful, nourishing gift she could give herself. It was easy to think of, and easy to do.

Stopping by her neighborhood church every day didn't threaten the fabric of Theresa's world. No one was shaken up by it. But Theresa's husband did keep asking why she was going to church so often all of a sudden. "I mean, it's fine with me," he'd say, "but I don't understand why suddenly . . ." Theresa too wondered if she didn't have a hidden agenda. There was a part of her that doubted herself. So you see, even in the easiest case, feeling fully entitled doesn't come automatically.

Some women know what they're going to do the minute they hear about the gift of a year. But that doesn't mean they haven't been considering possibilities. Theresa had been going along for years asking herself how her life could be more satisfying and meaningful. Every new possibility that came up—from disco dancing to the Internet—she'd considered. Knowing what she wanted to do with her special year happened quickly, but it was really the end of a long process. And that's how it should be.

The gift of *your* year has got to feel like a big deal to you. It's the equivalent of where you go to eat to celebrate your tenth wedding anniversary. Not McDonald's. Not your favorite everyday local Chinese restaurant, either. It was going to pray in church every single day that made the experience special for Theresa. That *was* a big deal for her. It was a radical change in the quality of her life, based on something she truly cared about.

And you always need *some* sense of how you're going to do what you're going to do. For Theresa, her plan grew out of a simple fact. The schedule of services and the schedule of her life weren't the same. Going to church only for services would have meant not going to church a lot of the time. Or it would've meant hard-to-implement changes in her own schedule. Either way she'd be setting herself up for disappointment or failure. So Theresa's "plan" was simply an attitude of flexibility—she'd go when she could and take what she got. That was a plan she could succeed with. Any time we make a plan that's flexible enough to hug the contours of our real lives and of ourselves, we will end up feeling successful.

Speaking of easy, you've probably figured out that the gift of a year has nothing to do with New Year's resolutions. Resolutions usually involve trying to make yourself do something you know will be hard for you—probably because part of you really doesn't want to do it. For example, you know the resolution to lose weight will be a battle, because you know how much you like to eat.

There should be no sense of struggle or any risk of failure with the gift of a year. You're doing something you've been wanting to do for a long time. It's about pleasure, indulgence, self-care, nurturing yourself, giving to yourself. It's about seizing the day for yourself so you can do something you've long wanted to do. It's not about making something happen. It's about *letting* something happen. It's not about pushing. It's about *stopping* pushing.

Here's another example of how easy the gift of a year can be. It's not about following the basics in some rigid, step-by-step manner. It's about knowing the ingredients that ensure that you'll have a successful year.

Amanda. When you're starting out as a couple, your house gets furnished piecemeal. But now Amanda hated the way her house looked. It was boring, ugly, and incoherent. She'd been too busy to do much about it. So Amanda decided that for her special year she'd gear up and then go ahead and do the job of refurbishing the major rooms in her house the way she wanted.

Again, this was an easy idea for her to come up with. It was easy for her to feel entitled. And it was relatively straightforward to put into practice.

Like a lot of women, the job Amanda did was not the work she dreamed of doing. Amanda worked as a legal secretary, but she'd always played with the idea of becoming a decorator, or maybe opening some kind of furniture or fabric store. All Amanda knew was that she wanted to do something connected with furnishings.

Now she and her husband were trying to have kids. Amanda knew that once the kids came it would be a few years before she picked up the threads of her own life again. "What a perfect time to give myself the gift of a year, and what better thing to do than fix up my house?" she told me. Three benefits in one. She'd have a full-scale experience of decorating a house. She'd begin the process of possibly becoming a decorator later on. And she'd indulge her desire to fix up her nest in that time before her babies came.

As for feeling entitled, yes, Amanda was lucky. Her husband's business was doing well, so they finally had some money for her to fix up the house. And they now could afford for her to work part time. Besides, her husband liked the idea of having a beautiful house, as long as he didn't have to do anything to make it happen.

As for fitting everything she wanted to do into a year, well, that was important. What if she got pregnant right away? She wanted to have it all done before the baby came. This meant that she couldn't wing it. But, hey, even making hamburgers requires a plan. If you don't have the buns and plates and everything ready when the hamburgers are done, they'll get overcooked or get cold. She knew that running around buying furniture would land her in the same mess she was in now—a new mishmash instead of an old one.

So Amanda was smart. She gave herself a full four months of her special year to read decorating books, to study the rooms in her house, to let ideas percolate, to shop around, to draw up plans, to get people's feedback on her ideas. By waiting four months before she spent her first dollar, she took the pressure off herself and made the process even more enjoyable.

At this point some women might say, sure, it was easy for Theresa and Amanda. But I have so many demands made on me.

And I have so many unmet needs and unfulfilled dreams. It's not so easy for me.

I'm with you. When I did my special year I was in your situation, not Theresa's or Amanda's. I needed to know that I could find a way to sort through the same issues you're sorting through. So don't worry. I'll show you exactly how to deal with all your concerns, just the way when I was starting out I would've loved someone to show me how basically easy it was to give myself something wonderful that I really needed.

The Easiest Special Year of All

It's your choice, but if I had to write one prescription for all the millions of women in America who need to give themselves the gift of a year, here's what I'd say. The women of America today are champs. We are as hard working and accomplished as women anywhere in the world or at any other time in history. But we are also some of the tiredest women in the world. So do whatever you want with your special year, *but start out for the first month or so giving yourself nothing but a really good rest*. A true and total rest is the one makeover women today need most. I'll bet you won't even recognize yourself once you get it.

Maybe you'll need a lot more than a month or two to recharge your batteries. Here's a woman who shows how the wonderful gift of a year is not about accomplishment, unless you want it to be. How giving to yourself has everything to do with it. And, by the way, how you never know what surprise you'll end up getting from your gift of a year.

Jennifer's Story

She'd been through a tough time. Jennifer worked hard, but that was okay. The problem was she'd been as unsuccessful in love as she'd been successful at work. The straw that broke the camel's back was that her third relationship in a row had just fallen apart. Three men in six years, and she had nothing to show for it but a tired and trampled-on heart. If there were a foreign legion for emotionally burned-out women, Jennifer would've joined.

Like most of us ready for the gift of a year, Jennifer needed something, and she needed it badly. At first all Jennifer knew was that she felt she needed to float in something warm and sweet, like a marshmallow in a cup of hot chocolate. For lots of women, this is the first way we see what we need: as an image, a feeling, a metaphor. Jennifer needed the space to let go, soften, and melt, just the way you might soak your weary feet after running around all day. Lots of women get to this place: the feeling that in some way you'd like to go check into a health resort and be taken care of for a year.

But there was a little more to it than just emotional fatigue. Jennifer needed—and this always plays a role—to place herself first in her life. For her that meant leaping off the mating merry-go-round. She needed to stop getting all wound up about finding some stranger to give her heart to and instead give her heart to herself for once. Amazing, isn't it? Sometimes the person we have to say *no* to if we're going to say *yes* to ourselves is a stranger we haven't even met. Jennifer needed to stop running after men she didn't know and start getting to know herself.

The year she needed quickly jelled in her mind. "Bubble baths and books!" she shouted, as thrilled as Newton when an apple falling on his head helped him discover gravity. Instead of coming home from work and running around in the hope of meeting someone, she'd take a nice long bubble bath and read a book. That was her gift to herself. As simple as that.

Jennifer badly needed to do this for a year. The point of it was not to take the occasional bubble bath. We do that all the time. The point was to clear away the space in her life that came with giving herself a year of bubble baths. And it had to be a firm decision, because part of her was spooked by the incredible daring she was showing by shutting down to men for one year. What if this was the one year Prince Charming happened to ride through her life? she wondered. What if she was somehow bringing herself bad luck, and if she said *no* for one year, guys would say *no* to her forever?

But the wiser part of her let herself enjoy her gift. As is always the case with a wonderful gift, there were a lot of unexpected surprises. For the first time in years she was sleeping well, because the long bubble bath before bedtime relaxed her as nothing else had done. The books she read were a big unexpected treasure. At first she read novels because that was easiest. But after a couple of months she found herself wanting to tackle self-improvement books and books on women and psychology. Before she knew it, an hour or so every night in a bubble bath turned into a kind of delicious self-directed reading program in which Jennifer learned about herself and what was possible for her in her life.

The most important thing she learned was that she liked and respected who she was and what she was doing with her life. All the energy she'd put into panting after men had somehow given her the illusion that work was a sideline, a stopgap. And of course all that did for her was make her feel that she was wasting her time ten hours a day.

Now she realized that she liked the work she did as a business broker, bringing people who were selling their businesses together with people who wanted to buy a business. She helped people's dreams come true. She brought a commitment to honesty to an area where not everyone was 100 percent honest. And the game was fun to play.

She'd felt so deprived. Yet the truth was—when she let herself feel it—that she liked her life and was proud of it. As her year of bubble baths flowed on, Jennifer realized that the most important thing that had been missing in her life was her own commitment to her life. Right now she was a business broker, and that was an honorable and an exciting thing to be. What she needed to add was excellence. Not that she wasn't a hard worker, but she could learn more about what she was doing and find new ways to do it better. That's what was on her plate right now.

As for men, the bubble baths taught her that being alone wasn't a nightmare from which she needed to be rescued by the first man that came along. Yes, when the time came she'd have to put out the word that she was ready to meet someone. But she felt she could now afford to be selective; to take things more slowly.

By the way, when she met the man she married, she connected with him because he'd read and loved two of the books she'd read in her bubble baths—*The Road Less Traveled* and *Angela's Ashes*.

Sometimes you have to take a detour to get where you always wanted to go.

The Courage to Claim What's Yours

Jennifer's special year was bathed in Mr. Bubble. Mine wasn't. Yours probably won't be either. But what all our different years share is an act of daring. I'm talking about the daring that comes from admitting what you want and doing something definite to give it to yourself.

That's what *your* gift of a year is. It's what you'll do every day, and most important, it's what you'll get as a result of what you'll do every day.

So when you give yourself the gift of a year, you wake up one morning, maybe tomorrow morning, and you know that every morning for an entire year you'll be able to look forward to something special, something different, something new added to your life. It could be something that takes five minutes a day, half an hour a day, an hour a day, or, if you're lucky, more of your day. It could be something you devote one day a week to. It all depends on your circumstances, and on what you want to do with your year.

When the soil of the self is exhausted, no beautiful flowers can grow from it. So make sure that your special year feels good and makes you feel good. If it does that, your gift of a year will be a big deal to you regardless of what else it does or does not accomplish. The key is taking care of yourself. That's the ultimate accomplishment. Because it makes everything else you can accomplish possible.

4

The Secrets of Success

*"Why should I feel confident I can give myself
the gift of a year?"*

I f you know anything about women's clothing, you know that whatever your shape or size, you can find clothes that can flatter your figure. There are *bathing suits* designed for every shape. How can this be? Actually, it's surprisingly easy. There are so many possibilities with fabric and pattern and cut that every woman can be accommodated.

It's the same with the gift of a year. We're all different, and our lives are different. And it's certainly true that our lives themselves bulge and pinch in ways that make you wonder if you really can give yourself the gift of a year. One woman has so many demands on her that she can't imagine clearing away some time for herself. Another woman wants so many things and yet has so much trouble figuring out what she really needs that she wonders how she'll decide what to do for her special year.

So sometimes it's natural to wonder, "Can I really do it?" The answer is: "Absolutely"—just the way you can find clothes that flatter your figure.

There are eight essential secrets that will make you fully confident that it's possible to give yourself a special year.

Revealing the Secrets

Let's use Jennifer's story to illustrate the secrets of success. You're different from Jennifer, but the essential secrets are the same for everyone. Just remember, though, what these secrets are all about: looking at your life with fresh eyes to discover new possibilities. That's important. We all start out with questions. But we also all need to start out with self-confidence.

Secret 1. *It's okay for you to think about what you could do for yourself for an entire year that would make you really happy.*

Jennifer had been running the race to find a man. She'd defined what she was doing in terms of survival and success—how can you manage in life or call yourself a winner unless you get a man? she'd thought. Particularly when all your friends have one.

Then Jennifer made an amazing discovery. Running this race didn't make her happy. On the contrary, the whole thing was just exhausting and confusing. We all have parts of our lives that we hoped would give us wings that for the moment have turned into something exhausting and confusing. If we're honest, this could be anything. Parenting—because sometimes kids are really difficult. Being on the fast track at work—because sometimes nothing's harder than slowing down on the fast track. *Anything.*

What you need in the midst of all this is something *big* that will make you happy. Maybe spending a year taking bubble baths doesn't sound big to you, but it made Jennifer happy, and the big thing it did was get her out of the man-chasing rat race.

How do you give yourself the gift of a year? You say, "Look, my life will take care of itself well enough for the next twelve months, but now there is something I can do every day that will make me happy, and I deserve it."

Imagine yourself a little old lady heading off toward Retirement Village, and on your way you think back on your life, smack yourself on the forehead, and say, "Damn! I forgot to be happy."

This kind of thing happens more often than you'd think. Happiness is a priority, but there are two other priorities we put first: survival and success. Yeah, we'd like to be happy but first we have to survive—and these days that includes work, childcare, shopping, investing . . . all the basics. Then there's success. Beyond surviving, we'd like to get ahead. We all define getting ahead a little differently, but we all have some sense of what it means to make it, what it means to somehow take another step with our lives.

Survival and success. For most of us, these—not happiness—are the North Pole and South Pole of our worlds. They are what keep us going like a sled dog in the Iditerod. It's because you organize your life around survival and success that doing something to really make yourself happy seems like it will threaten your world. It's not that we see anything wrong with being happy. It's just that we can barely devote enough time and attention to success and survival, so to try to be happy almost seems as if it would mean neglecting our priorities. At most, all we feel permitted to do is make a pit stop to fix ourselves up a little so we can continue to run the race.

But happiness is not the lowest of the three priorities. It's equally important. It's just the most postpone-able of the three. That's why we're in terrible danger of waking up one day and realizing that we've forgotten to be happy. And if you do wake up to that realization, it won't be much comfort to say, "Well, at least I survived and found a bit of success."

The first secret of women who make the gift of a year work for them is that they realize that it's okay to make happiness a priority now, today, before it's too late. It's responsible, not irresponsible, to give yourself a year that will make you really happy.

Secret 2. *The key to doing what you want is making room in your life for it, and there always is room in your life for it.*

It's a mistake to think you have to get everything all set up before you go. That may be true for a party: you have to put out food and drink before your guests show up. That may be true for making a cake: you have to line up all the ingredients before you make the batter. But it's *not* true for giving yourself the gift of a year.

Think of a different image. Let's say you want flowers in your garden. All you need to get started is an empty space in your garden in which to put flowers. Or a whole bunch of little pockets of empty space. First you create the holes, then you think about filling the holes. In fact, once you see the holes, your taste and knowledge and imagination will suggest to you how to fill them.

It's that easy to get started giving yourself the gift of a year. You start by giving yourself the gift of empty bits of time. Can you give yourself one whole Saturday or Sunday every week free from commitments? Can you give yourself half an hour just for you every morning or evening? Can you steal half an hour from work every day? Can you get your boss/husband/boyfriend/mother/kids/friends to cut you some slack?

That was all Jennifer did to get started. All she had in her head in the beginning was "Be less busy in the evening; save more time for me." Even the idea of using her extra hour or two to take a bubble bath and read a book didn't come until after she'd made that inner decision to have time in the evening just for herself.

I know time is a big topic for you. It certainly was for me. I remember a long period when it seemed like all I did was bounce back and forth between my patients and my children. They all needed every ounce of what I had to give. I didn't even feel I had time for my husband. It was as if I were surrounded by a wall of people who saw me as nothing more than the person who took care of them. Emotionally I didn't feel I had room to breathe.

I know how hemmed in we all can feel, and that's why I used to believe that under some circumstances you can't give yourself a special year. I used to believe that if you have a new baby or a tough new job, your time and energy are just not your own.

I now believe something very different. The gift of a year, more than anything else, is a state of mind. It's a way of orienting yourself. It's a kind of focus. It's where you say, "For this year I'm going to focus on getting something I really need that'll make this year one I'll remember forever."

Focus, not quantity of time, is the key. Someone once asked the cellist Pablo Casals how he was able to keep playing at such a high level for so many years. His answer was that early on he'd learned that no matter how fast the fingers of his left hand were flying up and down the fingerboard, after he pressed a finger down on one string and before he pressed it down on the next he would completely relax it, if only for a nanosecond. There he is working so hard, and on another level he's taking a vacation!

That's why you can always find time in your life. Because you can always find bubbles of opportunity to take care of yourself.

A *zero-time gift.* Let me introduce Caroline. She gave herself the gift of a year the very same year she started an incredibly demanding job running the claims division of an insurance company. She had less time than ever. But what she needed was to find a way to keep going with less stress.

Here's what she'd do. In the middle of a meeting or going from one task to the next or standing in the elevator, Caroline would close her eyes for a few seconds and say to herself, like a mantra, "You'll be okay. You don't have to worry. You can trust yourself. Even if you make a mistake, it will be all right." That was her gift of a year—remembering to use every moment when she wasn't actually talking to someone to stay in contact with that part of herself that remembered that she didn't have to live with pressure and anxiety. It was literally a psychic safety valve.

You see: *you can find time for yourself even if you literally have no time*. It just depends on what you're trying to do.

So if the question is how do you *start* giving yourself a year, the answer is find time somewhere, give it to yourself, and let your special year begin there. If you start with empty time, you'll find a good way to fill it.

Secret 3. *The best thing you can do for yourself during this special year is most likely something simple and basic.*

Let's face it, we all feel deprived. I've never met a woman yet who had only one thing missing in her life, only one unfulfilled desire. For most of us, if we suddenly had all the money and time in the world, there'd be a huge list of activities we'd be eager to take on. There's not enough money and time in the world to do all the things we'd want to do if we had all the money and time in the world.

Plus, let's face it, some of us want to live up to other people's expectations. The people in your life probably see you as a go-getter with all kinds of energy and ambition. So there's a temptation when you have a special year to do something impressive. One woman told all her friends that she wanted to do something special for her year before she knew what she wanted to do. And her friends said things like, "I bet you're going to learn how to play the electronic piano or hike the Appalachian Trail by yourself and write a book about it."

Suddenly this woman felt badly about herself. The kind of thing she'd had in mind was spending a year listening to classical music so she could reconnect to something she'd once loved. This wasn't anything that would impress anybody. You can see how we might be tempted to do more with our special year than make ourselves happy.

Jennifer just fell into her bubble baths, so to speak. It was bubble baths first, and doing it for a year second. But she had the right idea. How do you give yourself the gift of a year? Think of something doable. Something manageable. Something you'll be successful doing. Something so basic that your complicated life can't screw it up.

The women who had the best experiences with the gift of a year usually did something simple and basic. Okay, sometimes they did something elaborate and spectacular. But usually doable is best. You're always at risk when your eyes are bigger than your stomach.

Secret 4. *No matter how many people are clamoring for your attention, you can carve away enough room for yourself to get the gift of a year.*

Your life is not a conspiracy to squeeze you out of consideration. Some things you have to say *yes* to, but believe me, there are plenty of opportunities in your life to say *no*, certainly for just one year.

Here's an analogy. If you sleep in the same bed with someone, you can always get more elbow room—a nudge here, a little shove there, maybe a subtle kick or two, and the next thing you know you finally have enough room to stretch out. It's the same way with the gift of a year—who's going to give you the space you deserve in your life unless you claim it for yourself?

The key is saying *no* when you don't think you can say *no*. Most of our lives are so jam-packed that we don't have any easy *nos* available to us. All our *nos* are hard. So what? That's the beginning of freedom. Every woman who gave herself the gift of a year did so by tackling the tough *nos*.

This even applies to Jennifer, whose life had slightly more give to it. Do you think it was easy for her to say *no*? She had to say *no* to the voice inside her that said if she didn't run around trying to meet new guys, she'd be alone for the rest of her life. And, as she put it, "I had to keep the answering machine on too, twenty-four hours a day, because I had enough friends in crisis to keep me running around plenty, and I had to say *no* to them too.

"Look, it was only for a year. And I guess I'd basically told my friends I was going to be really busy with work, and I told some of the people at work that I was busy with friends in crisis, so I kind of got myself off the hook with everyone. But it was to save my life. I realize that now. The part of me that kept chasing men had gotten me into a lot of trouble. I'd panic at the thought of two weeks without a boyfriend, and then I was surprised because I kept getting involved with the wrong kind of guy.

"I'd never been able to say *no* to anyone before because I'd never been able to say *yes* to myself. That's what was so incredible about the aftermath of my special year. It wasn't so much that I'd gotten really rested and learned a lot from my reading. It was all about feeling empowered. I can do this, I thought. And I don't know how to explain it, but to me that meant I could do it forever. After that I owned my life."

How do you get a special year? It's like with drugs. Just say *no*.

Secret 5. *The people in your life want you to be happy.*

This secret is going to help you say *no* to others and *yes* to yourself. The world loves a happy woman. Remember Cameron Diaz in *There's Something about Mary?* It was her happiness most of all that gave her her magic.

And the people in your life are truly interested in your being happy. The confusing thing is that they don't go around advertising this. Your boss, your kids, your husband mostly talk about how they need this and they need that from you. But when you're unhappy, a part of their world collapses.

So if you have to shuffle your priorities around and put someone last who's been coming first, and some of the people in your life start giving you grief, just remember how happy they'll be when you're happy.

Jennifer was empowered to give herself the gift of a year in part because of her mother. In my workshops, I ask everyone to raise her right hand who feels that her mother was basically miserable. Usually most of the women raise their hands. I was surprised the first time that happened. Now I'm used to it, but it still makes me sad.

Just think about it. Most of us see our mothers as unhappy people. Maybe not on the surface, and maybe not all the time. But for every woman whose mother was basically miserable, her unhappiness created a barrier between the two of them. What we need to focus on is the lesson to draw from this.

So in my workshops I always go on to say, "Now keep your right hands up, and if you wish your mother had sacrificed a little less and done a little more to make herself happy, raise your left hand." Almost all the women who'd raised one hand are now raising both hands. Jennifer's mother was like this, a woman who wore her misery like a shawl. When women say I don't want to be like my mother, usually, more than anything else, they're referring to their mother's self-sacrifice-tainted unhappiness.

Well, just the way most of us wish our mothers had been happier, most of the people in your life want you to be happy. When you give yourself the gift of a year you're doing yourself a favor, and you're doing the people who truly care about you a favor too.

Secret 6. *Whatever you need or want, there's something you can do for a year that will give it to you.*

Some women fall into the cynicism trap. In many cases, the smarter you are, the more likely you are to fall into this trap.

The cynicism trap is this. You've run into your share of difficulties and disappointments in your life. You know how hard it can be to get back anything like what you put out. Of course this is painful knowledge. What we often do is deal with the pain of this knowledge by congratulating ourselves for how well we can size up the world. If you can't win by being hopeful, you think you can win by predicting the worst and having it come true. Now you win when you lose!

And so cynicism triumphs. This is a terrible trap because of the way it sets us up for even more disappointment. Our psychic energy gets tied up in imagining how things can go wrong, not in making them come out right.

Here's how this plays out when it comes to the gift of a year. Some women start out discouraged. The cynicism trap has led them to feel that the very things they might want most are just what they'd be least likely to get. They think they're protecting themselves from further disappointment by feeling this way. But they're really depriving themselves. You don't win when you talk yourself into the idea that good things are impossible for you. The secret of women who give themselves the gift of a year is they say, "Sure, my time, energy, and resources are limited. But if I let my desires be my guide, I can get some of what I really want."

What Jennifer really wanted was freedom, wisdom, peace of mind, and a good rest. That's a lot to ask for. But instead of acting like a wise guy and dismissing the possibility of getting this, Jennifer focused on what she could get by staying true to what she really needed. She understood the deep wisdom that getting some of what you really want is better than getting all of whatever it is you think you can get most easily.

So how do you give yourself the gift of a year? Assume there's room in your heart and in your life for you to get something big that you really want. (Chapter fifteen is all about how to turn big, deep needs into something doable in your special year.)

You can't get everything. And you can't get it perfectly. But if you have the courage to face life's inevitable limitations, you can get more than you ever dreamed of.

Secret 7. *If you know where you want to go, you'll know how to get there.*

Some women are daunted by the complexity of what they want to do with their special year. "I want to reawaken the artistic part of myself." "I want to see about starting a business of my own." These are daunting things to think about. Sometimes real planning is involved. And later I talk about how to plan when you absolutely have to.

But as Einstein said, the biggest step toward wisdom is making complicated things simple. Are you feeling daunted, overwhelmed, confused by what you want? Don't get lost in the details. Just ask yourself, "At the end of my year, what do I want to have for myself that I don't have right now?"

Here's the crucial step. If your answer is vague, make it specific. The key is being clear about how you'll *know* you've gotten whatever it is you want to get for yourself. Say you want to get in touch with the artistic part of yourself. How will you know you've gotten that? When you've produced a piece of art you're proud of? When you've found the kind of art you like doing? When you get to express certain feelings? When you've simply taken a serious art class? When you have artistic friends?

Yes, start with your dream. But then be very specific about some concrete, practical way that you'll know a bit of your dream has come true.

At first all Jennifer said was: "I want to take the pressure off." But then she realized that she'd feel less panicky about finding someone else if she first found herself. And finding herself simply meant relaxing, being quiet, and reading books that would help her think about herself. That was a clear destination. Once she saw it, getting there was easy.

To give yourself the gift of a year, just see clearly and specifically what you want to have at the end of your year that you don't have now.

Secret 8. *You'll enjoy your special year more when you realize you can have many special years in your life.*

Sometimes a woman gets stuck because she thinks, "Oooh, one, single, solitary year for me in my life. What am I going to do with it?" Yikes! That's an awful lot of pressure for one little year to take. Let's take the pressure off.

I have the same kind of problem when I go to a nice restaurant I've never been to before. I have trouble ordering from the menu. There's so much that looks good, and if I choose one thing, I have to give up something else. There are always a few moments when I feel stuck.

What gets me unstuck is remembering that I can come back to this restaurant. I'll certainly be going out to other restaurants. This isn't my last meal! Okay, suddenly the pressure's off. I can order what feels right in the moment and enjoy it. I can let go of all the other wonderful things I haven't ordered because I tell myself, hey, if this is really so great, I'll come back.

Well, who said you had to give yourself only one special year in your whole lifetime? In fact, many women find a way to do something special for themselves *every year.* So if this is your first time, be confident that it won't be your last time. You don't have to get every need met right now. You don't have to cram everything into this one year. You don't have to feel you're repairing your entire life to feel permitted to take this special year for yourself.

Relax and enjoy your gift by being confident you'll have many others.

You now know the secrets of women who've successfully done what you're about to do. The secrets all have this in common: relax, listen to yourself, trust yourself, keep things simple, have a specific idea of what you want, and know that you can get it.

5

My Story

"How did you come up with this idea?"

Saving My Own Life

L et me tell you how the gift of a year saved my life. But I have to warn you, my special year itself was as mundane as a pair of sweatpants and an old T-shirt. And I like it that way. The gift of a year isn't about grafting a propeller to the top of your head so you can fly around the room. It's about everyday people leading everyday lives with everyday needs. Water's nothing special either, but it can save your life if you're dying of thirst. The gift of a year is water to get us through our lives.

Okay, so there I was, a youngish woman trying to launch her career, and take care of two little kids, to say nothing of a husband who needed a lot from me. Who can't relate to that? No one would have looked at my life and seen anything wrong with it. Nor *was* there anything wrong with my life. Not in and of itself. And that's how we get fooled. There's nothing wrong with mashed potatoes either. But if that's *all* there is, there is something wrong. There's got to be more to life than just mashed potatoes.

I know what it's like. Any time I want I can close my eyes and remember back to what it was like to feel in my bones that all there is for me is go, go, go. Listening to other people until I can no longer hear them, no matter how hard I try. Feeling I'll scream if one more person asks me for one more thing. Lying in bed at night unable to sleep because my head and heart fill with thoughts of all the things I have to do, with all these worries floating on a rolling sea of my own needs that I don't even want to know about. Being grateful for those few wonderful minutes between waking up and getting up, the only time of the day that truly belongs to me.

Then one day I ran into Filene's Basement to buy some summer clothes for my kids and I bumped into a friend from college. We'd been close in school but had had no contact afterward. It's so easy to lose track of people. Anyway, we had one of those typical catching-up conversations that are fueled by curiosity and the desire to brag a little.

When we said goodbye, I found myself strangely disturbed. This woman had remembered me very well. Too well. She remembered all kinds of interests I'd had. Passions. Ambitions. Her conversation with me was full of questions like, "Do you still . . . ?" and "Did you ever do anything with . . . ?" My answer to all her questions was *no*. All those cool things I'd done or said I was going to do—they were all gone.

We sort of acted like, well, you grow up, and life takes over. But I was upset because she reminded me that maybe my life had taken over too much. Yes, now I felt like an adult, not a kid. But comparing these two times in my life, when had I felt more like a person? My honest answer was *then*.

I'd felt more like a person in college because then my plate was filled with things that were for me. In a way, that's what it means to feel like a person. You design your own menu instead of eating other people's leftovers.

Maybe this wouldn't have mattered so much to me, except that as a young therapist I was busy trying to help other people so they could find their dreams and live them. I realized that in a way I was a hypocrite. I was helping other people get in touch with what they wanted in their lives, but I was losing touch with what I wanted for myself, and I was going nuts in the process.

Missing in action. The truth was that something big was missing in the middle of this life I'd so carefully set up. What was missing was *me*. It was weird. There was so much in my life I cared about—and of course I really loved being a therapist. But on another level there wasn't anything in it I wanted just for me. It was as if my life had turned into a motel room and the truth was I could walk out of it without any sense that I was leaving anything of my own behind. A stranger could easily move into my life, and nothing would be different. I was happy *as long* as I didn't think about who I was and what I really wanted for myself.

That's when I stumbled on what I now know many other women have stumbled on, the idea of the gift of a year. Please remember, though, that we all do something different with this gift and that what was right for me to do with my gift probably isn't what will be right for you to do with yours.

Anyway, it was spring. I fantasized walking out the door, getting on a plane, and starting a new life. I had a perfectly good life with people I loved and work I respected, and in spite of that, the sinister combination of feeling overcommitted yet not seeing much of myself in my life was just too much for me. We all fantasize from time to time about starting over.

Somehow I managed to calm myself down. I realized that this was serious. I had to find an alternative between (a) doing nothing and going nuts or (b) changing everything and losing too much that I loved. And for all of us there always *is* an alternative between these two extremes. You don't have to throw the baby out with the bath water to save the baby from drowning in the bath water. Between the alternatives of doing nothing and changing everything, there's always the great alternative of finding what's wrong and fixing it.

Connecting to what I cared about. Anyway, that's when I realized I'd been feeling badly because there wasn't much of "me" in my life. But for all that unhappiness I'd never gotten specific. Bumping into my friend reminded me of the specific things I'd cared about or been involved in.

Just thinking about those specifics made me feel very hopeful. What I could do, and what I actually did, was write down a list of things I wanted to do over the next year. I wasn't thinking of some rigid time frame, but something like a rough twelve-month period felt right to me. And I didn't think of them as resolutions. Resolutions are where you vow to do really hard things that some part of you knows you'll have trouble doing. That's why we usually break our resolutions. The things I wrote down were inspirations. Treats. *Gifts*. They were all ways of giving myself permission to do something I'd been longing to do for a very long time. They were all things I loved.

I told everyone in my life about my "to-do list." I said that I'd already made commitments to do these things because I wanted my husband and children and family and friends to support me. I was afraid that if I said these were just things I wanted I wouldn't get anyone's support. Plus, I think I managed to somehow convey the impression that I was contemplating making some major change in my life, again so that people would take what I was doing very seriously.

The truth was that my year was a collection of treats. I took singing lessons for the first time in my life just so I could take it off my list of "things I've always wanted to do but never got around to." I loved to sing; why not sing well? Or at least better. And I spent more time with friends. I went for walks every day. I started reading again just for pleasure.

And I started keeping a journal. I'd lived my life as if I'd always be able to remember everything I thought, everything that happened to me, everything I felt. Ha! How little I remembered. Devoting a few minutes a day to a journal felt like a way to rescue a part of myself from drowning in oblivion.

Making it happen. To make sure I'd have the time to do what I wanted, I did things like create a fictitious patient, Hope Wright (check out her name!), whom I supposedly had to see every day. I'd write in my journal during my hour with "Hope." For the first time in my life I paid someone to clean the house. I not only got my husband to take up the slack, but I stopped paying attention to his way of doing things and figured at least I wasn't doing the work. I got up earlier and went to bed earlier. This didn't cut into my sleep. It gave me time, because when I got up early there was no one around to make demands of me, whereas at night I was busy with other people's stuff.

If you can give yourself a year, you can give yourself a life. For example, the time I spent writing in my journal—well, I never became a big journal writer. But I proved to myself I could stop the momentum of my life and take the time to say what I felt needed to be said. And that, five books ago, was how my writing career started.

An emotional hurdle. That's just some of what my special year was about. To tell you the truth, doing it was easy. But I was afraid it would be hard on me emotionally. Sacrifice was an important theme in my family. To be accused of being selfish was the worst insult, and it was a way my parents tried to control me. Any time I challenged what they wanted me to do and asserted my own desires, I was accused of being selfish.

Lots of us experience this. We're supposed to be selfless. "I'm a woman—I'm here to help." As girls we're trained to act this way by having our own desires labeled as selfish. No wonder we have trouble seeing what we really want.

So my fear of being labeled selfish was the emotional hurdle I had to overcome to get to the point where I could give myself the gift of a year. But when I actually did it, the things I did were natural. They were me. That's what made it so easy. How can you be selfish if you're being true to yourself?

I've had a pretty good life, knock wood. But for some reason I always look back on that year as my favorite year of my life so far. Some years in my life have been all about accomplishment. Some years have been all about taking care of business. Some years have been about putting out fires. But that year was about staking a claim to myself. That year I proved to myself once and for all who owned me. I owned myself. I belonged to myself. I was in charge of myself and my life. And all that came from giving myself a once-in-a-lifetime opportunity to experience myself and what I really cared about.

That's what made me wonder if I was the only woman in the world who'd given herself the gift of a year. It mattered to me. My whole professional life has been about helping women discover new possibilities for themselves, new sources of strength. So imagine how happy I was when I found other women who'd done what I'd done, except each did it differently and in her own way.

The Way We Can All Be

Here we are at the start of the twenty-first century, and some of us respond to the idea of giving ourselves a special year the way women at the start of the twentieth century responded to the idea of driving a car. "Really? Can I do that?"

It shouldn't be a big deal. So how come every woman in America isn't doing it already?

We live at a time in history when women are changing fast. In the past few decades women have changed more than ever before in human history. I've been a midwife to some of these changes, in myself, in my daughters, in the countless women I've worked with for twenty-five years.

I *like* the ways we're changing. But let's get clear about one thing. Being smart, tough, and capable is nothing new for women. Go back a hundred years, a thousand years, *ten* thousand years and you'll find mostly smart, tough, capable women. That's not how we've changed.

This new change is one of attitude. It's all about the sense that we're in charge of ourselves. No one owns us. I own myself. You own yourself. We choose our lives. No one touches us unless we want them to.

That's the attitude. "I'm in charge of me."

But inside, deep inside, it's a little different. "I have so many needs and dreams, and yet so few of them are reflected in my life." If you really are in charge of yourself, you should be feeling a little upset by now. Yes, you do what you want. *But have you chosen what you want?*

What we have today is a nation filled with what I call *the Wonder Woman marionette*. This a woman more powerful and more able to take charge than ever before in human history. But this is also a woman tied by emotional strings to the needs and rhythms of others. Super strong. Super tied down.

This is a paradox, but it's real, and I know you feel it. Too many women today are too much like this Wonder Woman marionette. But now we have the strength to cut our strings. And the gift of a year can help us do it.

* * *

It's good if you feel that something's got to give. You should be proud to feel that way. The more you feel something's missing in your life, the larger your self still is, the richer, the more you have to offer. You may be skinny on the outside, but you're big on the inside. It's like lassoing a wild horse: the more it bucks and kicks and struggles, the more spirit it has. We're all looking for ways to be free. The gift of a year gives you something wonderful to do, but even more important, it's an opportunity to be yourself, remember yourself, take care of yourself, and celebrate yourself, all at the same time.

DISCOVERING
THE PERFECT
YEAR
FOR YOU

6

Paying Attention
to the Real You

"What's a quick way to see what I need to do with my special year?"

Vivian. "Let me tell you about my inner stove. It's the biggest stove in the world. Hundreds of burners. On the front burners are all the *things* that demand my constant attention. But everything I'm cooking on the front burners feeds others, and a hungry lot they are. This stove that I'm chained to and keep dancing in front of is so huge you can barely see the back burners. That's where I've shoved most of the parts of me I care about. Things I want to do. Things I *need* to do, damn it. If I could just find a way to get to *one* of the things I care about that I've put on the back burner—it would be wonderful."

The easiest way to figure out what to do with your special year is to see what's staring you in the face and grab it. But how do you see the need or dream or desire that really is sitting there in front of you?

Let's look at your back burner. After all, a gift is no good unless it's something you want. The best gifts are things you've really wanted for a long time. The gift of a year is like that. It enables you to do what you've wanted for a long time. Like Vivian, we're not asking for much. We understand that the show must go on, that responsibilities must be met. We just want to find a way to also do something for ourselves that we care about, that has impact, that makes a difference, that feeds our souls. To give a gift to ourselves by rescuing from oblivion some long-ignored parts of ourselves.

Unfinished Business

So welcome to your back burner. We've all got one. We all go along doing first the things that are urgent. Your mother's coming for a visit, so you have to get your house ready. Quarterly reports at work are coming due, and you have to get your material in. Your best friend's wedding is in two weeks, and you have a lot to do. All this is urgent. Most of what you and I do from the moment the alarm goes off is take care of what has to be done sooner rather than later, immediately if possible.

In the middle of all that, you find yourself stopped at a red light and you look out the car window and see you're next to a playground filled with kids and the sun is shining on them. You used to be interested in photography, and you took some pretty good pictures, too. Now as you look at those kids you wish you could go back to taking pictures. You've had so many ideas. But no. There's no time. So you take that thought of doing photography and put it on your back burner. Some time, you think. Just not now.

When you get home that night you open your mail and there are your credit card bills, the monthly statement from your checking account, and the report from your 401k from work. Jeez, you think, I'd better start spending less and investing more. So you think, the first evening I have free I'll look at my finances. That starts you thinking about how you really would like to make more money, and what you'd really, really like to do is take some courses that will upgrade you at work. That's what you'd like to do for you. But first you have to balance your checkbook, pay bills, and put some money in your 401k. So there's one more thing—taking a course—you'd like to do for you that you have to put on your back burner because something else comes first that you can't even get to because of all the urgent things you have to do.

When it's time to rescue yourself. You can easily see how our back burners get overloaded with pots and pots of long-deferred needs and dreams. First you do all the things that have to be done immediately. Then when you can you do things that are important that you've put off doing, even though they may be things that don't matter to you deep down. They're just more responsibilities. Then and only then . . .

But then and only then never comes. Once they get put on the back burner, your needs and dreams never come off it.

But they never die either. Look—they're still there. Still warm. Still fresh even. Sitting there on the back burner are parts of you that will never die. And in many ways they're the most important parts. It's kind of nuts, isn't it? The things that occupy all your attention on the front burners keep you so busy—but they've little to do with the real you. And those things far away on your back burner, they are more you than anything.

Maybe you thought of turning your yard into a marvelous flower garden . . . but no, there are so many other things that have to get done first.

Maybe you thought of going into therapy . . . but no, it just didn't feel right to clear away room in your life to do that, even though you'd love to explore some issues from your past and get some advice about your present.

Maybe you didn't think of anything specific. It's just that there's this pot on your back burner that's had a lid on it for so long you don't know what's in it anymore. Inside you feel a kind of hunger for something. If only you could make it a priority to take the lid off and discover what you really want to do . . . but no, why bother? Would you do it once you discovered what it was?

And every time you say "but no," what are you saying "but no" to? *To yourself.* That's you, sitting there, on that back burner. That's more you than anything else. Isn't it? Which is *more* you: stuff your boss asks you to do or dreams of your own you've long deferred? Stuff your lover complains about or problems of your own? You know which is more you. And you know which you neglect. If you're not careful, before you know it you've put your entire self in little pots on your back burner.

Just reach out and grab it. The gift of a year might feel like a miracle. It might change your life. But at heart it's simple. *You take something off your back burner and put it on your front burner.*

If you don't, you could get into trouble. We can't take it forever, you and I, putting all these precious pieces of ourselves on the back burner. It's like if you forget to eat. Maybe you get so busy at work you miss lunch. It's one o'clock, two o'clock, and at some point it's driven home to you that there's no free lunch when it comes to missing lunch. Maybe you get a headache or feel faint. Maybe your mood turns sour. Your stomach hurts.

Then you explode into action. You find yourself feeding quarters into the candy machine because you're too hungry now to think about what you should be eating, what's good for you, what you need. More in need of nourishment than ever, you gulp down the empty calories of a Snickers bar.

The same kind of thing happens when you ignore the parts of yourself on your back burner. We hunger to take care of ourselves, and when we neglect that hunger, there's an explosion. We explode in frustration at having parts of ourselves slowly drying out on our back burners.

Stacey's Story

"Bob's the first thing I've done for me," Stacey said, sobbing her eyes out. What's this "Bob" she "did" for herself? Stacey was happily married. She had a job that she liked. But, as is true for millions of women, there was no Stacey in Stacey's life. It was all about being there for others. Stacey didn't have a clue what she needed, but she knew she was dying out there on the back burner. So she had an affair with this Bob she met while traveling for work.

Bob didn't give her much. There were more problems than benefits from being with him. Their relationship was doomed anyway. She didn't want to divorce her husband. But a starving woman will grab for anything.

Women like Stacey have always haunted me. A woman with a marriage she wants to protect sleeps with a man she doesn't like as a way of dealing with needs that go untouched anyway. I call it the *Madame Bovary syndrome*. A woman's self is put on hold, she's starved for something, but she doesn't know what. In a state of desperation she grabs at what's available to her, not what she really needs. Emma Bovary with her love affairs was in a way nothing more than a starving woman who ate candy bars until they killed her. In her case and in Stacey's case they were the candy bars of infidelity.

When we've put too much of ourselves on the back burner, we end up gulping down some kind of candy bar to give something to ourselves to make the hunger of unmet needs and dreams go away. Is shopping for clothes your candy bar? Getting lost in an endless succession of novels about how women find romance? Picking fights with people close to you, because you're unhappy anyway and some kind of intensity is better than facing your real hunger?

Identifying What's on Your Back Burner

If there's something you've always wanted to do, you know it, don't you? If there's some nagging problem that's been gnawing away at you for a long time, you know it, don't you? All you need is to give yourself a chance to reconnect with whatever you've been needing and wanting for a long time.

To prime the pump, try completing the following sentences.

"Something I've always wanted to do is _____."

"What I used to really like that I haven't done in a while is _____

_____."

"I've been complaining about _____ for such a long time it's time I did something about it."

"I keep saying I need _____ now's when I should do something to get what I need."

Believe me, if you have something on your back burner, you'll have a way to complete at least one of these sentences. And then there it is. Right in front of you, you'll see what to do with your special year. Or at least you'll see something definite that gives you a hint about what to do with your special year.

Molly. Like so many of us, Molly had felt vaguely drained and disconnected for quite awhile. When she complained to her best friend, Molly would say things like, "I wish I could just walk out the door and take a boat somewhere for a long time." That wasn't what was on her back burner—that was just her way of expressing how she felt. She wasn't literally going around yearning for a boat trip. She didn't know what she was yearning for.

As a first place to look, I suggested to Molly that she check out her back burner. Sometimes the reason we can't see what we want is not only because it's so far away on our back burner, it's because what's on our back burner feels so out of sync with our lives as we're currently leading them. It's that discrepancy, not only the distance, that makes our back burners seem so far away.

Molly was a high school English teacher, a good one too, the kind that gets to know her students and cares about them. But even the best of us get burned out from time to time. Molly had done a whole lot of giving, but what had she gotten for herself? Back when she was in high school she'd wanted to be a total rocker chick. She'd been turned on by groups like Bananarama and the Bangles, by women like Pat Benatar and Deborah Harry and Cyndi Lauper. From time to time she'd see something on TV about novelists or lawyers or doctors who formed a rock group, and they'd always made her very jealous.

Her image of herself as a lead singer for a rock group was wildly discrepant from the person she was every day for her students. It was one thing to be cool and to be someone teenagers could relate to. It was another thing to act like the kind of person she'd warned them about using as a role model.

This is one way that parts of ourselves get stuck on our back burners: they don't fit nicely and easily into our lives. But they're vitally important for us to express if we're going to feel fulfilled.

When Molly saw what was on her back burner, she said to me, "Okay, I'll do it. This will be the year I get into a band. I'm in my thirties. I can still sing great. I look good. I just want to do it. I know I'll hook up with someone. What's the worst that'll happen? I don't care about not being a big success. The worst is that I'll actually get a gig and one of my students will see me. One of my students' parents will see me! So what? I'm not doing anything illegal. They'll just see me having fun doing what I love."

That was her gift of a year. Molly lived near Boston, so she had many ways to troll for opportunities. It turned out to be a fantastic year for her. It took about five months to hook up with a band. They had a fun, eclectic approach, covering a range of material from the Archies to Van Morrison to Bob Marley. They weren't making any money yet, but making money wasn't on Molly's back burner. "It's just about the music" happened to be true for her.

Molly's special year is ending. She's deciding what to do next. The band takes lots of time, but it's the most fun she's had in her life. She'd do music full time except she thinks the band won't ever make any money. Life is full of choices. Better to have choices. If Molly decides that the end of her special year is the end of her singing with the band, she'll still have memories she'll treasure. Perhaps most important, Molly knows she's done it; and that gives her a sense of triumph and confidence. Once you've rescued a lost piece of yourself from your back burner, you always know you can do it again.

If you don't know what to do with your year, look on your back burner. There it is, sitting there, what you've been wanting that will make your year a real gift. What feels better than getting something you've always wanted? Particularly when you can rescue what's best about you in the process.

7

Find Your Acorn

"What small shift will provide a major benefit in my life?"

ome women are lucky—they have more ideas for what they'd like to do with their special year than they can do in a lifetime. The problem is how to choose? If out of all the possibilities you're considering you don't know which to choose, ask yourself which one might have the biggest impact on your life.

It's All about Leverage

Being able to stake a claim and put more *you* in your life is very exciting. Being able to do something for a whole year that makes you feel good or feel nourished is very exciting.

But here's what I think is *most* exciting about the gift of a year. You can get a lot for a little. There are things you can do with your special year that can have an enormous impact on how you feel about yourself or on how you live your life or even on the direction you take with your future.

So as you think about what you want to do with your gift of a year, I invite you to *find your acorn*. Look for something to do that may be small in itself—in our crowded lives it may be hard to find room for anything but a small shift—but might have a big impact. That's your acorn.

Just think of the power of an acorn. It's tiny but it contains all the genetic information and other substances it needs to almost automatically transform itself into a giant oak tree. Many women find that the innocent little thing they do with their gift of a year has a similar impact. Yes, do what you want. Do what gives you pleasure. That's what comes first. But be on the lookout for the way small changes can have large effects.

Take Jennifer. It's hard to imagine a smaller shift in anyone's life than taking bubble baths every night. But Jennifer listened to herself and trusted she'd get what she needed. The oak tree that grew out of her acorn was the sense that she was sufficient unto herself. She didn't *need* to be with a man to be happy. She didn't have to panic about finding a man. She still wanted to find the right person and spend her life with him and have kids. But the panic she'd felt that had pushed her into making bad choices was drowned forever in those bubble baths. Talk about big changes growing out of small shifts!

Here are other women who got enormous benefits from the acorns they gave themselves for their special years. Seeing how they found small shifts that had big impacts will inspire you to find good ideas of your own.

Linda. We all know we need to exercise. But for most of us it's a real battle to fight laziness and busyness to the point where we actually do. Linda had fought a good battle, up to a point. A half hour in front of the television on an exercise bike four nights a week is nothing to be sneezed at. (I wish I could do as well.) Still, she had a hunger for something more. One day while pedaling away Linda clicked past a show on weight training for women. No, not female body builders. Linda found them a turnoff. But these weight-trained women looked great. Womanly but strong.

That's for me, Linda said. And that was the gift she gave herself. She shifted around the priorities in her life a little so that she could actually go to the gym four days a week and do some serious weight training. Less boring pedaling at home, more pumping iron at the gym.

She loved it, like a duck loves pond water. This really is for me, she thought, but she didn't know exactly what that meant. Then it hit her. She'd complained about her job as an office manager for such a long time that her husband and friends were all sick of it. But she'd stayed because it wasn't *so* terrible and mostly because she couldn't think of anything else she wanted to do. But halfway through her year of weight training she thought, "I love this. I'm good at it. I'm interested in it. I can do this for others."

Linda decided to take courses and do whatever else was necessary to qualify as a personal trainer. That was her new vision for what she'd do for the rest of her life. And it all came from the acorn of a decision to spend her special year weight training herself into shape.

Sometimes we're surprised at what our special years lead to. But sometimes there's something you think of doing, and it just beckons to you, and you're not sure why you're so drawn to it. It may be a sign that you've intuitively found your acorn. This specific gift of a year—seemingly innocuous—has the potential to lead to something big, and you know it. *Trust that feeling.*

Debbie. If you're the parent of a sick child who's in a hospital, you might find it comforting to know that your child's nurse is a worrywart. You'd see her as conscientious. Debbie was just such a pediatric nurse. A heroine to her patients, Debbie was a torment to herself. She felt that her constant worrying, not just about the infants in her care but about everything in her life, would one day drive her crazy.

The strain she lived with made her leap at the idea of giving herself a special year. To understand why she did what she did with her year, we have to go back to her childhood. She'd always been interested in science. For her tenth birthday Debbie talked her father into buying her a gigantic aquarium she wanted to fill with many beautiful fish. Debbie got the whole thing going, but then through overfeeding she killed all the fish. Maybe she shouldn't have felt so guilty, but Debbie felt as badly as if she'd destroyed a world. She lost the confidence that living things would automatically thrive in her care.

Now, years later, needing to give something to herself but not having much time, Debbie decided to try the aquarium again. This time she'd do it right and her miniature world of beautiful fish would live. You may not know fish—I certainly don't—but evidently, in the limited time Debbie had, it took her a year to set the whole thing up, make sure it was stabilized, and bring it to a thriving state—a beautiful self-sustaining miniature world. After all, an aquarium is a total balanced environment with not just fish but plants and organisms that can clean up debris in the tank.

Mastering that miniature world that was in her control was a wonderful experience, but it gave Debbie a lot more than simple pleasure. Success was actually easy. Understand what the fish need, don't overdo it, and trust them to take care of themselves. And, yeah, even with the best of care every once in a while a fish dies and there's nothing you can do about it. One day, watching the fish swim around, it hit her. "All they need is for me not to screw things up for them. I don't have to overdo it."

That's how Debbie found her way toward peace of mind as a pediatric nurse. Before she'd felt she had to do her own job and Mother Nature's as well, because she was afraid to trust her infants to Mother Nature. Now the fish reminded her that all she had to do was her job, and she could trust Mother Nature to take care of the rest. Debbie found a way to see herself as a healer and a creator, not a destroyer, and so she stopped worrying.

If you or I should decide to set up an aquarium, we probably wouldn't take from the experience what Debbie took. But that's the point of finding your acorn. It's *your* acorn. Based on your life history and psychological makeup, it's the unique seed that will bring forth a new you.

Debbie didn't know what would come of setting up an aquarium. She wanted to do it because she wanted to do it. She simply followed what resonated for her in her heart. Not knowing what an acorn will grow into is one thing. You don't *have* to know. Having the sense that what you want to do is some kind of possible acorn that has the potential to turn into something—that's something you can feel.

For example, I didn't start keeping a journal with the idea in mind that it would lead to anything. When I was a kid I used to write all the time, and even in high school I'd fantasized about becoming a writer. But I hadn't thought I was good enough. Where I'm similar to Debbie is that what I did during my year healed some unfinished business from my past and so put me on a new course as I moved into my future. I didn't know that would happen when I wrote in my journal, but I listened to what I wanted to do and trusted that it would be good for me.

Helena. Sometimes success can be a dead end, and it was that for Helena. She'd first gotten into computers because she was struck by the power of computers to change the world, and she wanted to be part of that. But you know how it is. Your abilities and the opportunities the world throws your way drift you into strange channels. Helena had ended up designing computer games, and she was actually rather famous for it in her world.

But hers was a very small world. It was mostly inhabited by the kinds of guys who were nuts for computers and computer games. Other than the fascinating work itself, there wasn't much in that world for Helena. She was lonely.

It bothered her that she wasn't able to help more people who needed it. "Maybe the way to help people isn't through my work with computers," she thought. Helena decided to give herself a very special gift. All that pressure at work—screw them. They needed her more than she needed them. Twelve-hour days to come up with more vivid ways for cartoon characters to kill each other was ridiculous. Helena decided to give herself the gift of one year in which she'd work less and find some way to help people who needed it. Maybe she couldn't keep it up for more than a year, but at least she'd be able to look back and point with pride at what she'd done.

She began by checking out possibilities. This is always daunting for someone who wants to help people, because there are so many people in the world in need of help. How do you choose? But for some reason Helena got turned on by the work of Amnesty International. She was no bleeding heart, but the idea of prisoners of conscience being tortured or kept in horrible conditions got through to her. And she knew that political pressure often made a big difference in helping these people. Somehow she felt that computers could play a role in this, because of their ability to link the world and lift people out of darkness.

So Helena volunteered herself. To make a long story short, by the end of her year she felt she'd played a small role in rescuing four men and two women from endless imprisonment by setting up web pages and Internet connections. And she'd given hope to many more.

But that wasn't the real miracle the gift of a year gave to Helena's life. She'd expected to help people. What she hadn't expected was that she would let *herself* out of prison. Without even realizing it, Helena had given up hope of breaking out of her isolation. But the people she worked with at Amnesty International became a real community. They became her friends. Now she had people who liked her for who she was, and she liked herself with them.

Her acorn was spending a couple of hours a week helping others. That was worthwhile in itself. In terms of its emotional impact, the oak tree that sprang out of this was her sense of belonging to a community. That's one of the things about acorns. Sometimes all you know is that it's a seed. What it turns into is a big surprise.

Nancy. A wise woman once said, "You can have it all, but it gets messy." That's how Nancy, a bank loan officer, lived her life. With two kids, ages four and six, Nancy figured she'd get by as long as she was willing to put up with a certain amount of chaos in her life. So she ran around all the time and left a lot of jobs half finished. Who said you had to be perfect?

Like most women, Nancy needed to feel she could find some room in her life for herself. She had a vague idea of what the gift of a year would be for her, but she had a very specific way of getting it. Although their money was budgeted, she got her husband to agree to hire a part-time nanny, just for the weekends. Just to give Nancy a little room to breathe two days a week.

She envisioned it as a kind of half-vacation every weekend for a year. That was her special year. It was better than she thought it would be. Instead of going from the frying pan of work to the fire of her weekends, Nancy had time to enjoy herself on her weekends. She could sleep a little later, enjoy her kids a little more, go and do things with her husband, and see friends. It felt as if she'd been walking around with a fifty-pound weight on her back and suddenly all that weight was taken off.

After a couple of months of basically resting and de-stressing, Nancy started getting bored. There were a lot of loose ends at work, and she'd been longing for a way to feel she was getting on top of her job. So she used some of her newfound time first to clear up the backlog and then to redesign her job.

Out of the acorn of a few free hours on the weekends grew a whole new way of thinking about her job—what she did and how she did it. She found ways to delegate, to create computerized forms for doing reports she'd had to rethink each time in the past, and to streamline processes she'd thought couldn't be streamlined. Sometimes we're so busy, it's impossible for us to see how inefficiently we're working. That's what had happened to Nancy, and that's what the gift of a year saved her from.

What you actually do with your special year might be small in itself. But if it's something important to you, expect it to have a big impact on your life. When you're thinking of what you want to do with your special year, do whatever feels right. But let yourself be guided by whatever hunches you might have—they just might lead to something big. Look for something big to happen. If you feel at all that some part of you is suffocating in your life, you don't feel that way because of something tiny. You might not have to do anything big—that's the beauty of acorns—but you surely need something meaningful to come from what you do.

But don't get stuck here. Don't worry about finding your acorn. Don't run around searching for your acorn. And don't spend a minute looking for the perfect acorn. Just do what feels right. Do what beckons. And then simply be prepared to be surprised when something big happens.

8

The Ten Dream-Discovering Questions

*"How do I dig down to find what
I really want in my heart?"*

Welcome to Your Heart's Desire

ow can you know what you want to do with your special year if you don't know what you want, period? Uncovering your deepest needs and desires is an important way to point yourself toward knowing what your gift of a year will be.

When I do workshops helping women give themselves the gift of a year, we always get to the point where it's time to talk about what they want to do with their special years. I ask the women in the room to sort themselves into three groups. I'll say something like, "If you know exactly what you want to do with your special year, go stand on the left. If you have a vague idea of what you want to do but you're just not sure how to do it, go stand on the right. And if you just don't know at all, go stand in the middle."

Which would you guess is always the biggest group? Over and over, with an amazing consistency, the biggest group is the women in the middle who don't know what they want to do at all.

Over the years I've learned something about this large group of women in the middle. They may not know what they want, but they sure know they want something. I've asked these women—and you may be one of them yourself—to talk about what's simmering away on their back burners. Sometimes it's hard for them to start opening up, but once they do, their needs and dreams and desires just pour out.

Toni. I'm thinking particularly of Toni. I think the first impression any of us would have of Toni was that she was mousy. Her clothes were brown. Her hair was brushed very flat on her head. I found out that she was a librarian, a single mother with two children in elementary school.

"What do *you* want, Toni?" I asked her. "Make a guess."

"I don't know," she said. "I'm here because I know I need time for myself, but I don't have anything really in mind for what I'd do with that time. Maybe I just need time to do nothing. I could sure use a rest."

"Well," I said, "that's exactly what lots of women need. In fact that's the first thing I usually tell women to do with their gift of a year. Get some rest. But you've got to be open to the possibility that there's more. Maybe a lot more. Do you ever have daydreams about what you could be doing with yourself? Or maybe you're aware of something that's holding you back in your life that you'd like to tackle. Just talk about what you used to like to do or what you think you'd like to do."

Toni stood biting her lip for a moment. Finally she said, "I don't know where to begin. Well, starting at random, I was on the swimming team in high school. I love swimming. And I daydream about that, but I want to do it, you know, seriously, not just show up once in a while at the Y. In college I played golf a lot. I always daydream about playing golf. But you know I daydream about having a farm. I daydream about having a farm where troubled kids come and they get helped just from working on the farm. I daydream about traveling to the most faraway places I can think of. I daydream about studying art and really knowing all the painters and when they painted and why they're important, maybe so I could be one of those people who give talks in museums explaining paintings to the public. I always thought that was great . . ."

Toni started out not knowing what she wanted, and before we knew it she could barely stop her flow of dreams and desires.

That's what it's like for a lot of us. Next time you're out in public and your eye settles on some not very remarkable looking woman, remind yourself that within that plain brown wrapper may lie the most amazing dreams and aspirations you can imagine. Not *just* dreams and aspirations either—given half a chance, a woman like Toni can do amazing things.

How did Toni finally go from not knowing what she wanted to knowing exactly what she wanted? She answered my famous ten questions. If you don't know what you want to do with your special year, answer these ten questions, and you will know.

Here's where the magic in these ten questions comes from.

The evidence is solid: *what we "really" want is the same as what we've "always" wanted.* Freud was right here—nothing is more satisfying than the realization of a childhood dream. Particularly if you interpret the word *childhood* as including adolescence and even early adulthood.

Time ripens desires. It validates desires. Maybe you sort of feel like eating a cookie right now. If you get distracted, you'll most likely lose your desire for that cookie. It didn't stand the test of time. But when there's something you want that you've kept on wanting for a long time, even if you've forgotten how much you want it, then that's something you *really* want. And that will be something that will really satisfy you when you get it.

The miracle here is that old desires are often some of our most easily satisfiable desires. All that's happened is that they've gotten lost in the shuffle. Like a piece of paper on your messy desk you could easily take care of, except that it's gotten shoved to the bottom of the pile.

So let's go on a treasure hunt. *Answering these ten questions has shown women their buried dreams and therefore has given them the possibility of seizing a chunk of time that's based on what they really want.* What's worked for others will work for you.

Don't strain your brain. These questions are easy to answer, if you just let yourself say the first things that come to mind. Don't worry about your answers being "right." They're right if they're true. And don't be afraid that your answers commit you to anything. Their only function is to lead you through the trunks in the attic of the self to help you reclaim buried treasures.

You don't have to sit at a table with a pen in your hand. That's not comfortable for some women. But you should write down your answers once they've come to you. The point is to let yourself ramble and daydream. You might have to come up with a number of answers to a particular question before you see the one answer that turns you on. And you can keep adding to your answers. I envy your being able to experience answering these questions for the first time. It's a lot of fun.

Welcome to seeing to what's best in you.

THE TEN DREAM-DISCOVERING QUESTIONS

1. *What are seven of your happiest memories?*

Sometimes your most important unmet need is to recapture a form of happiness that once was yours. Memories of situations in which you were happy can point you toward ways you need to change your situation. For many women the perfect year is one where you do again what once made you very happy. Remember if it brought you joy before, it will bring joy again.

2. *What were your dreams for your future when you were younger?*

Surely you haven't fulfilled all your dreams. And the most satisfying dreams to fulfill are the ones with the deepest roots. It certainly doesn't have to be a dream for how you're going to completely reshape your life. It might just be a dream that will add something new to your life. Too many of us are afraid of our dreams. Don't be. Even if every dream can't come true, there's no better guide to what's missing and what you now need than your dreams.

3. *What do you like best about yourself?*

This is a time to really give yourself credit for what's best about you. It's a mistake how much energy we put into shoring up the weak spots in our personality. I think we should put at least as much energy, if not more, into building on what's best about us. So maybe you can do more with what's best about you. Please admit the truth; don't think of it as bragging. Knowing what you like best about yourself isn't about thinking you're wonderful. It's about tapping into what gives you the greatest satisfaction.

4. *What kind of life would you lead if you had ten million dollars?*

No, this isn't designed to tantalize you. It's designed to lift you out of preconceived limitations about what's possible for you. When it comes to bringing your dreams to light, this question can be very effective. Maybe you can't literally do with your special year what you would do if you had ten million dollars, but knowing what it would be can point you toward something you can do.

5. *Name some things you'd most enjoy doing—I'm talking about fun and pleasure here—that you're not doing right now.*

What better principle than the pleasure principle to help you find your dreams? The women most in need of the gift of a year are usually the women most likely to neglect giving themselves genuine pleasure. The barrier to get through here is being able to admit what really *really* gives you pleasure. A lot of the time we get the most pleasure from doing things that we wouldn't want to boast about. Guilty pleasures. Lonely pleasures. Weird pleasures. But these may be just what you need most, and because they're hard to admit they may be just what you have least of in your life right now.

6. *When you look at the world around you, of all the things you feel connected to, what would you most like to change or improve?*

Sometimes the best gift to yourself is a gift you give to something you care about in the world. This question gives you the opportunity to see if that's true for you. Let's make one thing clear: you already do plenty for other people. This is for you, but it's for the part of you that wants to give to people who don't have an immediate claim on your time. I think we all have a deep psychological need to feel that what we do matters. But the fact that something matters to you doesn't mean that it necessarily matters to a troubled world. The shortcut to the sense that you matter is doing something that shows how you care about the world.

7. What has given you the most fulfillment so far in your life?

You don't have to reinvent the wheel. If something has given a lot to you before, it might be best to turn to it again now when you're needing to get something for yourself. The key to answering this question successfully is to give yourself time to think about it: some of the deepest fulfillments take the longest to bubble up to the surface when you're looking for them. If something worked once, why won't it work again?

8. Who are the five people who are your biggest role models?

I once knew a highly accomplished woman who guided herself through life, whenever she came to a turning point, by appealing to her inner Katharine Hepburn. "What would Katharine Hepburn do here?" she'd ask herself, and then she'd always know what to do. Most of us contain within us the images and voices of people who are guides for who to be and how to live. But sometimes we get away from what our inner idols would want for us. Knowing who your top five role models are, seeing which one you've gotten furthest away from, and figuring out what to do to win back his or her approval can be a wonderful way to be true to yourself, to be proud of yourself, and to come up with a great idea for the gift of a year.

9. What are three things you want to change about yourself?

Many women decide to use their special year to focus on one specific part of themselves they want to improve. By naming three things, you give yourself the sense of having options. But don't feel you have to "go deep." Some of the most important, satisfying changes we can make in ourselves are on the surface. It's more important to focus on a change that's specific and doable than on a change that's "deep" but vague and difficult. Once you pick something you want to change, your idea for your special year comes when you know what to do to change it.

10. *What are five things that are most important to you that you have the least of in your life right now?*

I'm talking more about the spiritual than the material end of things: more time with close friends, more peace of mind, more fun, more self-understanding. The best way to come up with five things is to come up with twenty-five things that are important to you that you have the least of and then pare your list down to the top five. Then maybe you can use your special year to get all five. Maybe you'll have to choose one.

Let yourself experience the real, hard, bottom-line, stark-naked truth as you answer these questions. You're not out to impress anyone. Just answer the ten questions honestly. And if you haven't really let yourself tell the truth of your gut (as opposed to the truth of your head), take another stab at it.

From Answers to *the* Answer

Now look at what you have. We all end up with answers that point in a number of different directions. How do you find *the* answer?

• Maybe it just jumps out at you.

Maybe one answer to one question stands up on its own two feet and shouts, "I'm the one! Do me!" Great! You've found your answer. You suddenly have a clear sense of what's missing in your life that you can do something about. Now all you need to do is check out some of the possibilities so you can see the best way to translate your sense of what's missing into a special year in which you give it to yourself.

• Maybe there's a pattern to your answers.

There may be some variety, but most of them keep pointing in the same direction. Lisa found that many of her answers pointed to the desire for peace. Not world peace, although that's certainly desirable, but inner peace. Peace in her daily life. Some of her happiest memories had to do with the peace of long country walks. The peace of quiet Sunday afternoons. The peace there had been in the house when one of her parents was gone so they weren't fighting.

When she thought about how she'd live if she had ten million dollars she thought about living on an island or turning the day upside down so that she was awake at night when everything else was quiet.

Lisa was a kindergarten teacher, and she always said she loved her work. So it had disturbed her when she found herself filling with a vague unhappiness and a longing for some unnamed escape. Lisa was afraid that whatever it was that was missing would require some kind of revolution in her life to set right. Lisa was like a lot of us: she knew there was something wrong, yet she also knew that a revolution in her life was not the answer.

The idea of "finding peace" was the key she was looking for. When she started her special year she *didn't know exactly* what that would mean for her, so she experimented. She was a single mother with two teenaged kids; she told them she'd been under a lot of strain and needed "rest" so she wouldn't have a "nervous breakdown."

Then she went to bed early every night so she could get up early every morning. After all, the early morning is the most peaceful time of day. She took up knitting, of all things, because she'd learned how peaceful it was to do from her mother. In fact, when Lisa was in the midst of her family somehow the fact that she was knitting calmed everyone down and made them act more peacefully toward her. How can you hassle a knitting woman?

Lisa's example shows something important. If your answers to the ten questions point in some clear direction, go with it, even if you don't know exactly what to do yet. As long as every step you take is a step in that direction, your year will be a gift.

◆ Maybe your answers don't point in one clear direction.

That happens. What that means is that you've suddenly generated what probably seems like too many options. You want to go swimming and you want to take guitar lessons and you want to garden and you want a master's degree and you want to throw lots of dinner parties and you want to travel throughout Europe and you want to make a lot of money . . .

You could spend the rest of your life exploring the pathways you've just uncovered. You're overwhelmed. But in fact you're much closer to finding what you want to do with your special year than you might think.

Okay, so you have all these ideas, based on your answers to the ten questions. Here's how to funnel a pot full of ideas down into the option that's best for you. But be prepared—we're going to move fast.

Translate each of your ideas into completions of either of these phrases:

+ "I'd like to spend the next year of my life doing nothing but . . ."

or

+ "I'd like to spend the next year of my life focusing on . . ."

Some of your ideas will drop out because you can't find a way to translate them into completions of these phrases. For example, maybe one of your happiest memories was recess back in elementary school. But you can't see how to put hopscotch and Double Dutch jump rope into your life now. Not all signposts to happiness can turn into the gift of a year.

You'll still have a number of ideas left. Now, simply look at them and eliminate all but five. I don't care how you do it, but just do it. Be ruthless. Just get down to five. The five best, of course. Define *best* as most easily doable and most likely to be satisfying as you live your life now.

Look at your five ideas. Why not do all five? Challenge yourself with the question, "Is there any reason I can't fit all five of these wonderful things into one wonderful year?"

Here's an example of someone who did just that. In one year Cammy, a hard-working publicist, spent a week on a ranch, went for a four-day trip to the shore with an old friend, wrote a notebook full of songs, took the time to listen to all the music she loved, and started taking tennis lessons once a week.

But maybe you want to focus on one thing. Can you pick one out of the five? If so, problem solved. You've got your year, or at least an indication of your focus.

Can't pick one? Then eliminate one of the five. Just force yourself to do it. Then eliminate another. Just do it. Okay, now eliminate one more. You've only got two ideas left. Give yourself twenty-four hours. If it's not clear by then which one you want to do, flip a coin and let fate point you in the right direction. We don't always have to rationally choose. Sometimes what's best for you appears by chance.

Every time I talk about the gift of a year to a group of women, there's one person who knows exactly what she wants to do down to the last detail the minute she hears about it. I always have mixed feelings about this. I hope I'll always be first in line to champion women following their dreams. But it's a little like knowing what you want to major in in college. Some of us go off to college knowing exactly what we'll major in. Some of us start out knowing exactly what we want to do after college. You don't want to squash that. But I support attempts by colleges to expose students to a wide range of possibilities before they commit themselves to a major.

All I'm saying is: "You can know what you want based on how you feel. But how can you know you'd feel the same way once you know what all your options are? Otherwise, for example, we might as well all marry our high school sweethearts."

The ten dream-discovering questions help you see what's real inside you. Now over the next few chapters give other women a chance to open your mind and heart to new possibilities.

What's the worst that can happen? You'll start out knowing what you want, and in the end you'll be sure you were right.

Every woman who's said "I want to put more me in my life" is really talking about her buried dreams. The part of you that can't breathe in your life is almost always some buried dream. Don't be afraid of your dreams. A dream really is nothing but a way of knowing what will make you happy. What better way to know you than to know what will make you happy? Welcome your dreams—there's no better guide for navigating through life.

CONSIDERING
NEW
POSSIBILITIES

9

A World of Possibilities

"How can I see the full range of possibilities for my special year?"

ee if you can imagine all the different things women have done with all their special years. I'll bet that even if you have a very vivid imagination the range of what's possible will surprise you. It certainly surprised me.

Most of us feel we don't have a lot of wiggle room in our lives. Yet as the stories started coming in, I was amazed at some of the things women did with their special years. Talk to your friends and share ideas. You'll be amazed at what they come up with for you and for themselves.

But the point isn't to be impressed. The point is to expand your sense of what's possible for you.

Love Story

It's the oldest story in the world. Boy meets girl. Boy loses girl. Boy finds girl. Happy ending.

That's the basic structure behind every love story. Well, you have a relationship with yourself too. The story of your relationship with yourself should be a kind of love story too, shouldn't it? It certainly shouldn't be a hate story. And for most women it is a love story. Girl meets self. Girl loses self. Girl finds self. Happy ending.

Where are you in this story? Somewhere in the middle, probably. That's where most of us are. We are roaming around that long middle, that starts in adolescence, where the self is lost and is trying to look for itself. As Dante said of himself in the first words of the *Divine Comedy*:

In the middle of the journey of our life, I came to myself in a dark wood, for the straight way was lost.

He was in his early thirties at the time.

I don't want to overstate this point. None of us is completely lost. For many of us it's only a small piece of the self that we've lost. The piece you've lost might be as small as the need to get a good rest. But unless you're able to take care of yourself a lot better than most women, the piece of yourself that's gotten lost, however big or small, is an important piece. You miss it terribly. Plus, how can all of you feel safe when part of you has gone missing?

The gift of a year is specifically designed to help us bring home these missing parts of ourselves. The following four women did very different things with their special years. Their stories are just an introduction to understanding what's possible for you to get for yourself.

Abby. Figuring out what you want to do with the rest of your life. "I felt like I'd spent my whole life on someone else's escalator. I'd studied business in college because it seemed practical. Then I took the first good job that was offered me—not because it was something I was burning to do but because it was there, like an up escalator.

"Then it entered my head that there may be something I really wanted to do with my life, something that came from me. I wanted to build my own escalator, and I wanted it to go where I wanted it to go. Of course I tried to figure out what I really wanted to do, but my days were filled with so many responsibilities that I could never tune in to the still small voice within me that knew what I wanted all along.

"So I turned a corner. I told everyone who'd made claims on my time that I had some big decisions to make and that for a period of time they'd need to let me alone a little so I could think about them. It was really the same 'you'd better back off a little' speech we've all used from time to time for different reasons. Then what did I do? Nothing earth-shattering. I talked to people who could help me sort things out, including a couple of career counselors. I went for walks. I read books that made it possible for me to explore new avenues. The point was that this was my year to slow things down in my life so I could figure out where I wanted to go next.

"Because I was focused, because I'd shut out so much noise, I could really listen to myself for the first time in years and years. I hadn't been able to do that before because everyone else had been making so much noise with all their demands. And in a little while I realized that I wanted to become a nurse. Ideally a midwife. I'd never really been all that interested in making money. I'd always wanted to help people—that's what I really wanted to do. Talk about being a midwife—in that year I spent thinking about my future it's like I was pregnant with new possibilities and then gave birth to myself. I just needed the time to focus on and connect with what I really wanted."

Abby did something big and deep. But don't be misled by this. That's what Abby needed; other women needed, and got, very different things.

Jessie. Recharging your batteries. "I'd been giving to other people for so long. To say nothing of what my job took out of me, which was in commercial real estate, so it was push, push, push. And then a month after I turned thirty I broke up with my boyfriend, or accepted his breaking up with me, or whatever you want to call it. I'd cried a lot just over the whole turning-thirty thing, so breaking up was just the icing on a big, crappy cake.

"Talk about running on empty. That was it. I had nothing left. It's like I'd spent my life chasing stuff and trying to keep it alive by pumping it up with my own energy. Well, screw it, I thought. I don't have it to give anymore, and I don't even want to give anything to anybody. At least not for awhile.

"It wasn't like I sat down with my appointment book, but I just sort of felt my way to a decision that I needed something like a year to lie fallow. I mean, I still needed to work to eat, you know, but even there I was like, hey, for one year—nine to five, and that's it. The rest of the time I wasn't even going to chase a bus. I needed a year to do nothing. I thought of it almost like convalescing.

"I had no plan, but I had a goal. Every day I would do something special for me. I mean that if I just wanted to stay home and watch a movie on Saturday night even though my friends proposed all kinds of plans to me, I'd do it. If I wanted to wander down to the Y and swim for an hour, I'd do that. If I wanted to take a drawing class or a yoga class, I'd do that. I actually did a lot of things, but in my mind at the beginning I told myself that if I did nothing more than come home from work every day, get into bed, pull the covers over my head, and lie there until morning, that was okay and I would damned well do that if I wanted to."

You know how it is with a gift. Sometimes the best gift is something you've really really needed for a long time. That's what Abby and Jessie got. But sometimes the best gift is something you don't need at all. It's something completely extra. Or maybe I should say that sometimes what we need most is precisely something completely extra. A total detour that caps off your life in a way that nothing else can. It doesn't have to lead to anything, or connect to anything. All it does is make everything wonderful and utterly change how you feel about your life.

Nina. Having an adventure. "In one sense I had everything I wanted. My kids were great, and they were cruising along through school without much need for the heavy-duty involvement I'd put in when they were little. My husband was happy-go-lucky. And my work as a dentist was really a dream job, what with my involvement at the university clinic and my teaching there and everything. The nightmare part of this was weird. I wanted everything I had exactly the way I had it, but the thought of it just going on and on forever without changing scared the crap out of me. I didn't want my life to change, but I wanted some change in my life.

"I realized that it was up to me. If I didn't do anything, things would go along without any change. I'd be an old woman and wonder where my life had gone and why I didn't have more interesting memories.

"But I'd always had a dream. Africa. My roots. Where my people came from. I didn't want to do the whole Alex Haley thing, but I'd always dreamed of traveling right to the heart of Africa, the Congo or some place like that, not as a tourist, either, but sort of living there with the people. I knew they'd think of me as an American, not as an African, but I didn't care. I just wanted to experience it for myself, something about what life was like for my people before the beginning of the African experience in America.

"But of course I'd diddled along and I hadn't sunk my teeth into it. Because, let's face it, your dreams won't come true unless you make them a priority, and that means you've got to do something that maybe makes some people a little uncomfortable and shakes up their routine just the way you're shaking up your own. But how else do you get a year as special as the year I wanted? So what if everyone said that I was the bad woman who left her family to go to Africa for a year? Hey, I'll come back, you'll get over it, I said, and no one will get hurt. You'll forget, and I'll get something I'll never forget."

These three women gave themselves special years that involved going outside of their everyday lives. But not every gift is like that. Imagine one day being home by yourself painting the inside of your house. Suddenly a friend shows up ready, willing, and able to help. That would be a gift indeed. Well, in the same way, sometimes the best gift is one that gives you something you need to cope a lot better with your current life. After all, the gift of a year isn't something taken from your life. It's a gift for your life.

Kate. Finding a way to get on top of your life. "When I got the promotion it was like a dream come true. To me marketing computers is very exciting because it's a way to change the world. I'd always been part of a team, but with my promotion I was captain of the team. I was in charge of an entire product line. I knew it would be tough being captain of the ship—the buck stops here, and all that—but I figured it was going to be about making decisions. Instead it was really about being responsible for everything. Instead of having to fit ten hours work into an eight-and-a-half-hour day or something, it felt like I was trying to do thirty hours of work in a twelve-hour day.

"I was overwhelmed and overburdened. My big fear was that, with everyone looking on, I'd just collapse. 'No one can do this job,' I thought in despair. But somehow that flipped it around, and I felt a lot better. It was true. No one *could* do this job. Which meant that all I could do was try and cope. It wasn't about being perfect. It was about learning how to not stress out.

"So I said to myself, look, I'm not going to worry about being excellent anymore. If I just survive, that's plenty excellent for me. What I am going to do is give myself a gift. Okay, Kate, I told myself. You've got one year, and all you have to do is one simple thing. Figure out how to sail through this job without getting your feathers ruffled. My gift to myself was a year to focus on doing my job without stress. All I wanted by the end was to be able to say to myself, 'Maybe you weren't perfect, maybe you weren't wonderful, but you were *cool*.'

"To be honest, I felt scared and guilty going into my special year. Was I just being lazy and irresponsible? Here I finally get this big job, and I focus on how I feel. But that's what I needed to focus on. If I didn't make taking care of myself my top priority, there'd be no job, no me, no nothing. I'd just be a basket case.

"It was the best decision I ever made. Everything I did that year, everything I thought about, was about discovering the least stressful path. So I survived. I delegated. I found ways to share responsibility. I discovered shortcuts. I learned there was a whole bunch of things I could just ignore. I learned I didn't have to obsess about unfinished business.

"I didn't run a perfect ship, but I learned to be totally cool running it. And guess what? I was an enormous hit with my bosses. The computer business is chaotic anyway, so they didn't expect smooth sailing. But that I could cope so well and seem to take everything in stride—that knocked them out."

Four women, four stories. It's just the tip of the iceberg. As varied as women are—that's how varied the ways are that women have given themselves the gift of a year. Maybe you want to get on top of your life, maybe you want to escape your life. Maybe you want to find a way to have fun again, maybe you want to start getting serious. Maybe you want to improve yourself, maybe you want to find yourself. Maybe you want to focus on one thing, maybe you want to focus on a bunch of things.

But I don't want to overemphasize the differences among the things women did. There were also two common threads. No matter what you do with your gift of a year, no matter what it does for you, there are two things all women get.

- New options
- A new sense of yourself

The world becomes richer and you become richer to yourself.

Millie captured the hunger for *new options* that we all feel.

Millie. "I've been doing the same thing for a while now, and it's okay, but I'm starting to wonder if this is all there is. I have this strong feeling that I'm bigger than my life, like my life is a piece of clothing I've outgrown. It's like when you go to the same restaurant all the time and the food is okay but you're bored to death by the menu. You want new stuff to choose from. I just don't want to spend the rest of my life wondering if this is all there is."

You can't change what's possible for you without changing you. When you do something new or do something old in a new way, you're a new person. Every time you shake things up there's *a total revolution in your sense of yourself*. Martha expresses this beautifully.

Martha. "I always liked traveling, but I'd always traveled as an outsider. Because I only spoke English, basically. I knew it would be a big deal if I learned Spanish. I could go to South America and Spain and be more a part of things. So for one year I completely stripped down my schedule to the minimum and put every spare minute and every spare penny I had into learning Spanish.

"Well, you'd be amazed at how much you can learn if you really throw yourself into it like that. I know I was amazed, because I'd sort of thought, well, I don't have a talent for languages. But after a year I was reading Spanish newspapers and talking Spanish to people, and here's the difference it made to how I felt about myself. If I can learn Spanish, I thought, I can learn Italian, Russian, Chinese. I have the power, the potential, to talk to anyone in the world in their own language."

The Four Kinds of Years

To help you see the full range of possibilities for your gift of a year, the next four chapters break them down into four main categories for you to consider.

In the first category, *Just a Little R & R*, the gift in your year has to do with recuperating, resting, sweetly doing nothing. It's all about recharging your batteries, as it was for Jessie. You might not get bragging rights, because you won't be accomplishing anything you can point to with pride, but so what? The rest of your life can be about accomplishment. This special year can be about taking care of yourself so you can have those accomplishments.

The second category I call *Getting It All Together*. This is where the gift in your year has to do with being more effective, more organized, more successful, more *accomplished* in your life. I don't just mean your professional life the way it did for Kate. It could be your personal life. From career development to psychotherapy, from learning to manage stress to learning to manage a corporate division—in this category you give yourself a gift of self-improvement.

In the third category, *Where's the Rest of Me?* you explore yourself, and you uncover new dimensions, new inner potential. My special year fell into this category, as did the year of Abby, who decided to become a midwife. This is the category that's launched when you look at your life and say "There's more to me than this" and then you go on to find what that *more* is. And maybe take steps to make it happen for yourself.

The fourth category, which I call *Beyond the Blue Horizon*, is where the gift in your year comes from adding a whole new piece to your life. You have an adventure. You do something you've never done before, or something you've long dreamed of doing. Don't be misled, though. Doing something completely new doesn't necessarily mean having an exotic adventure, as it did for Nina when she actually took her trip to Africa. What's new for you, what your dreams are, is the key here.

As you check out all the possibilities, the most important thing is to have fun. Imagine going to the biggest and best mall in a part of the world you've never been to. You'd want to check out everything. Let yourself do that here. But be open. You may not know what the perfect year for you is until one of the women you're about to meet shows it to you.

10

Just a Little R & R

"I need to recharge my batteries: how can I devote my special year to doing that?"

S ome of the strongest women can get into a weakened place in their lives. Some of the most energetic can end up feeling the most tired. As a result, some women who need R & R the most get it the least. Here's why.

A lot of who we are is tied up with our *image* of who we are. Most of us strong, energetic women know we're that way. Our self-esteem, our very identity, is tied up with being strong and energetic. I know I'm like this, and I've paid a big price for it. It's the price we pay for not realizing we need to take care of ourselves. Recently, I got sick. At first it was just a cold. I kept working. Then my cold turned into strep throat, for which I took antibiotics. I still kept working until I collapsed. But even that wasn't enough for me.

In bed, unable to move, I plunged into a miserable depression. It was so *not me* to be weak and sick in bed that I felt obliterated. It was as if I'd lost my self, and it was gone forever. I was depressed because I thought I was doomed.

Here's where the message of this chapter comes in. Neither my strep throat nor my feeling depressed were necessary. If I'd admitted at the very beginning that strong, energetic women can temporarily feel weak and tired, I'd have taken better care of myself when I first caught cold, and even if I'd gotten strep throat I wouldn't have added to my misery by getting depressed about it.

I got better in a couple of weeks. But multiply what I went through by ten or twenty or thirty, and you have the life situation a huge number of women are in today. They're running on empty— *we're* running on empty—and we can't admit it even after things go seriously wrong. The price we pay is enormous.

The French have an expression: *Reculer pour mieux sauter.* This means that you have to step back, retreat a little, if you're going to successfully jump over something. Want to jump across a ditch? You don't just walk to the edge and then leap. You walk to the edge, gauge the distance, and then retreat a bit to give yourself room to get a full running start before you leap.

That's the function of this category of special year. And it's important to see it that way. When you need to rest and regroup . . . hey, you need what you need. But the point I want to emphasize is why you need it. *It's not because you're weak or lazy.* It's because you've been running on empty and you face important tasks. Sometimes we can't take the next leap forward unless we take the time to step back first. Where will you get the strength to *sauter* (leap forward) if you can't allow yourself to *reculer* (pull back)?

This issue is so important that I strongly urge every woman who gives herself the gift of a year to find ways to recharge her batteries first, whatever else she does afterward. And the reason this is so crucial is that you and I have an incredibly hard time admitting how truly drained we are. By the time we're forced to admit it, we're in pretty bad shape.

What's Your Battery Juice?

Whether you need a few weeks of R & R or a whole year, you must open your mind to a whole new awareness of what R & R really consists of. If you think it's just about lying in bed reading magazines, think again.

Rest doesn't mean doing nothing. It means lying fallow, and that means restoring the nutrition you've lost. It's about building yourself up. *Reculer* means retreating so you can advance. And retreating carries with it all the implications of a religious retreat—a way to spend energy to get more energy.

Recreation doesn't just mean enjoying yourself. It literally means re-creating yourself. It's almost a way of taking yourself apart and putting yourself back together again so that you feel better and function better. And so that you've worked out some of the glitches in your system.

R & R can be pretty profound when you realize some of the dimensions involved. This is key. As you think of giving yourself the gift of a year, it's incredibly important that you open your mind to some of the possibilities that exist in the area of R & R.

Let's explore some of these areas.

Physical. How do you know you *don't* need a complete rest for an entire year? Just because you say you're okay, just because the sheer momentum of your life sweeps you along, none of that means that you wouldn't benefit from going to bed and staying there for the next twelve months.

Not literally, of course. Unless you have a trust fund and servants, you couldn't stay in bed for a year even if you wanted to, and even then it would get pretty boring. No, when I talk about a complete rest for a year, I'm talking about working within the structure of your life as it exists. You probably have to go to work. You probably have a family and responsibilities.

But you'd be amazed at how much sheer physical rest you can get even in the context of *you gotta do what you gotta do*. As with every other form of the gift of a year, you make it a priority. You have one clear goal in mind. For one year you'll say *yes* to rest and sleep every single opportunity you can. And you'll say *no* to everything that gets in the way of rest and sleep. I'm talking about pretty basic stuff. Sleeping in every Saturday and Sunday morning. Going to bed early every night. Giving yourself a half-hour nap in the middle of the day whenever possible. Just as important—and remember this is just for a year—when someone suggests you do something and there's the chance that it will interfere with your getting your rest, you refuse to do it.

I've seen women benefit most from this right after they've gone through a particularly exhausting stretch in their lives. For example, the first year after your youngest kid starts school. A year after you settle into a demanding job. As soon as possible after a divorce or a death in the family.

You don't get bragging rights to a year in bed. That's the only drawback. But if you've run out of battery juice, there will be no spark unless you get some rest. And it's that spark you provide to your life that does give you bragging rights.

Emotional. You have to recognize the possibility that *any situation that stimulates your emotions can exhaust you emotionally.* And any situation that forces you to clamp down on your emotions can exhaust you emotionally. A lot more things are emotionally exhausting than you might think. The classic situations that make us think of emotional exhaustion include going through a divorce, a bankruptcy, a stretch of unemployment. Any major loss that involves fear and struggle. These situations leave us drained emotionally and in need of something special.

It's very important not to overlook situations that are just as emotionally exhausting but that we don't think of in this category. Working hard for a promotion. Getting married and settling down to a life with a new person. Moving to a new part of the country. Sending your last kid off to college.

How do you give yourself R & R when what you're suffering from is emotional exhaustion? Of course, going into therapy is an obvious option. But check out what women have said they've done that works. Most of these either you can do for a year or they can take place intermittently over the course of a year.

* *Casual traveling.* Maybe you can't travel for a year, but if you're emotionally exhausted you can spend a year doing the kinds of traveling that recharge your batteries. Going to a spa. Hiking and camping. Going to the beach. Taking driving trips. The key is to do the kind of traveling that makes you feel rested and rejuvenated, not the kind that leaves you more exhausted than when you started out. Adventures and visiting twelve cities in eight days are not for the emotionally exhausted.
* *Shopping.* That's right, shopping. Why not? When you're emotionally exhausted, you need to give to yourself. Why not over

the course of a year replace your furniture and your wardrobe, if you enjoy that and you can afford it and it rejuvenates you?

♦ *Getting into a new relationship.* Serious new love affairs are not what I'm talking about here. I'm talking about a new relationship that's fun. I'm talking about getting involved with someone where you enjoy yourself and each other without getting caught up in demands and expectations. Maybe it's just about sex. Maybe it's just about doing things together that you both enjoy, like dancing. Maybe it's just about talking.

See if you and your friends together can come up with other ideas for using the gift of a year to deal with emotional exhaustion. The key to all these is doing something that feeds you emotionally. How do you know your special year will do that? Here's a checklist. If what you want does *most* of the following and doesn't violate any of them, you're on to something that will rejuvenate you:

♦ Does it give you alone time or time you feel is just for you?
♦ Does it make you feel safe?
♦ Does it put you in a situation where you can express yourself?
♦ Does it make you feel supported?
♦ Does it help you break out of your sense of being trapped?
♦ Is this truly a way for you to give to yourself?

Spiritual. What does it mean to be spiritually exhausted? This is important because spirituality means so many different things to so many different people. What all the different forms of spiritual exhaustion have in common is the deep sense that you've run out of answers. The old answers don't work, and you can't come up with new answers.

Answers to what? To the questions that are personally meaningful to you. We're spiritually exhausted when we don't know why we're doing what we do anymore. When we don't know what to do next. When we don't know the meaning of what we're doing. Did you ever go to the store and when you got there you forgot what you needed? Suddenly you didn't know why you were there. That's a taste of spiritual exhaustion.

When you've run out of answers, you have to be careful. The

world is filled with answers. Everywhere you turn there are people ready, willing, and able to give you answers. That's not the kind of R & R you need. What you need is an experience that will allow you to come up with answers on your own.

That's why a religious retreat is a solution to spiritual exhaustion when you've run out of answers about your relationship with God. You go to a place where you know those answers exist. You participate in discussions and meditations and ceremonies. You get quiet inside and you open up to what's outside. Answers come flooding in. That's the kind of R & R you need when you're spiritually running on empty.

Ruby. Here was a singer who'd sung one song too many. It's hard to keep having the feeling when you keep singing the same words. The music had turned into empty words. Ruby was spiritually exhausted because repetition had brought her to the point where she'd forgotten why she was singing.

Like everyone who's run out of answers, she'd already gone through a period of pushing to find answers. "I just need a rest," she kept saying. And she'd take longer and longer vacations. It was as if she thought by not singing she'd reconnect to the meaning and passion within her songs. But this is important: getting some R & R may or may not be the same as simply getting a rest. That's why you need to find out what juices your batteries. You need to do more to a battery than simply leave it alone to fill it up with electricity again. You have to fill it with what it needs.

To recharge spiritually, you need to put yourself into a new context where you can get new answers. That way you can get plugged in to something that has the power *you* need.

When you've run out of answers, you often have to look in a completely different place. Probing the music itself for new inspiration stopped working for Ruby. Rest wasn't the answer. For her, R & R consisted of learning to have fun again.

"I can't believe how long it's been since I've really had fun. There's no fun in my life! It's not just that I work so hard and get so tired, but I don't have a fun attitude anymore either. There's a grimness about what I do and a grimness inside me too. And that's lousy because I know I have a real capacity for having fun. I'll always treasure this year because I learned how to play again. I did stupid things that had no meaning other than the fact that they made me happy. Of course, in the process I stopped thinking about singing."

Here are some of the things Ruby did to reenergize herself spiritually so she could keep her music alive. She did a lot of singing for children in schools and in hospitals. She traveled around the Caribbean to listen to people singing songs in their native context. She sang at weddings. She even did a stint as the tambourine girl in a friend's rock band. All these were just ways of having fun for Ruby. Here's what she got.

"In the end I discovered a new reason to sing. I'd always done these serious ballads and folk songs that I'd thought were so deeply meaningful. I think I just got burnt out on that. I'd forgotten, or maybe I'd never realized, that singing is supposed to be a pleasure, first and foremost, and the pleasure starts with the singer. I'd stopped feeling the meaning in the words because I needed to find new words and new meanings."

Ruby attacked spiritual exhaustion at its root. And you can too.

The most important thing about R & R is that if it's not based on what you truly need and how you really work, it won't help. Imagine two women; both feel drained. To rest and recuperate one needs solitude, the other needs friendly human contact. One needs to do nothing, the other needs to do new things. One needs to nourish her body, the other needs to nourish her spirit. R & R is about what you get for yourself, not what you do to get it. It's got to give you what you really need. Whether it's to discover what's best about you or to allow what's best about you to flourish, a year of R & R is the one thing to do when you can't think of anything else to do. It's always wonderful.

11

Getting It All Together

"I've got to get on top of my life: how can I devote my special year to doing that?"

ou're on top of your life when you do well and you feel good. If you're not doing well or you're not feeling good, you're not on top of your life. So whenever you and I need to get on top of our lives, it has to do with not being as effective as we'd like or not feeling as satisfied as we'd like.

Who among us doesn't find herself in this situation: the busier you are *having* a life, the more likely you are to fall behind *in* your life?

There are several different ways that women find themselves in the situation of needing to get on top of their lives.

• Some women need to make a decision.

Big decisions take time. You need to step back from your life to make one. It means getting information. Talking to people. Mulling things over. Once you make the decision, you have to carry it out. How many of us, for example, stay with jobs we hate because we're so busy on the job we can't take time to think about where we want to go next, much less actually search for a new job.

Is there some important decision you've been needing to make that you've been postponing? Why not consider giving yourself a special year to pull together everything you need to finally make that decision and do it right?

◆ Some women need to do better on the job.

We can put so much time into doing everything we have to do that we don't get around to doing much of it really well. There's always some piece missing that stands between where we are today and the success we know we're capable of. But this doesn't have to just be about our jobs. In your love life, in your exercise regimen, anywhere—doing everything you have to do can keep you from doing your best.

Is there a way you've been needing to do better in your life that you've been neglecting doing anything about? Why not consider giving yourself a special year to improve your performance in some crucial part of your life?

◆ Some women need to get strong.

As our lives go on, most of us realize that there's something we should be bringing to the table that we're not. It could be a kind of inner strength, it could be a better memory, it could be a kind of upgrading of our skills.

Is there some inner resource you've been needing to acquire that you haven't made time for? Why not consider giving yourself a special year to acquire this inner resource?

◆ Some women need to find a way out of *the chaos trap.*

Remember Kate, the computer marketing executive, who needed to find a way to do her job without getting so stressed about it? Nothing makes you feel more that your life is on top of you instead of your being on top of your life than feeling constantly stressed out. But the reason you're stressed out is that things have piled up and you're juggling so many balls in the air that you're completely disorganized. But to get organized takes even more work, and that's even more stressful. That's the chaos trap. Disorganization breeds stress which breeds the inability to cope with disorganization which breeds more disorganization which breeds more stress. Yikes! Anxiety attack!

Okay, now, breathe deeply into this paper bag—it's not so bad. This is just the kind of thing the gift of a year was designed to deal with. There is a solution. You just have to look for it.

Is there some important way you've been needing to get more organized that will make your life less stressful? Why not give yourself a year to do your job in a way that's more organized and less stressful?

Now, how do you use the gift of a year to get on top of your life?

The Gift of Effectiveness and Satisfaction

If you're feeling like your life is on top of you instead of your being on top of your life, you've got to ask yourself *why*. Assume that the reason is something very specific.

Good news: big problems can have small causes. For example, we've all had mornings like this. You wake up with plenty of time to get to work. And you have your morning routine down to a science. But something happens to glitch up your routine, and you fall behind, and before you know it your whole morning is a disaster. It feels as if the roof has caved in. But here's the interesting part: it's only one small glitch that's caused all the trouble. You had trouble starting your car, or your mother called as you were leaving reminding you to buy her pears.

Most women who use the gift of a year to get on top of their lives start by saying, "I hate my life." Fine. That's how you feel. Now you have to identify why. The more specific you are, the more likely you are to find a special year that will change everything for you.

You Know It or You Don't

Right now, most women fall into two categories. You either know what you need to get on top of your life or you don't. If you know what you need, what's stopping you?

Getting what you know you need to get on top of your life.

Where most women get stuck is that they actually know in what area they have to get on top of their lives, and they know what to do about it, but for some reason they have trouble giving themselves permission to do it.

Often this is caused by the fact that you and I have a false sense of the idea of balance. We all need balance in our lives. That's a given. Work and play, friends and family, romance and finance all must be given their due. So far, so good. The problem comes when we put too much on our plate and then insist that everything still has to balance out. It's simple arithmetic. *When you're overcommitted and insist on balance, everything gets short shrift. When one thing needs special attention, you can't pay attention to it if you're insisting on balance.*

This is a message women who are trying to get on top of their lives need to hear. The good news is that there's one simple thing you can do to end your stuckness and get on top of things. The challenge is that when you focus on that simple thing you may create less balance in your life in the short term.

But what did you expect? If you have to clear off an incredibly cluttered desk, and you have to devote a Saturday to that, that's not having a balanced life. If you pour all your energy and attention into a new baby, that's not having a balanced life.

Well, when you give yourself the gift of a year that will make it possible to get on top of your life, you're giving birth to a new you. Knowing that should make it feel worthwhile to say, "If I have to put parts of my life on hold for a year to get on top of my life, that's a good deal."

The year Heather said no to almost everyone. "I'm strung out," Heather confessed to me. "I've got too much on my plate. My big fear is that I'm not going to be able to handle it all. This year all I want is to learn how to get through it all with less stress, more efficiency. I want to know I can be good at what I do, and I want to know I can do it without having to pay too high a price."

What was bothering Heather so much? She wasn't on top of her life because she wasn't on top of her job. She wasn't on top of her job because she couldn't delegate. She couldn't delegate because most of her employees weren't up to speed on what they needed to be able to do so that she'd feel comfortable delegating to them.

But Heather could never take the time to get her employees up to speed because that would mean saying *no* to her husband, her children, her friends, her parents, and other people in her life who were already feeling Heather wasn't giving enough to them.

Everyone was saying, "Pay attention to me. Make me more a part of your overall balance." And the more she tried to maintain an impossible balance, the more her business was getting away from her.

Heather owned a small restaurant—the Blue Cat Cafe. A homey, clubby, hang-out kind of place. It was known for its food. And it wasn't really a small place. For that restaurant to run well, a lot of things had to run well. But Heather was the only one who knew how to do every job perfectly, from making dinners to making desserts, from running the dining room to managing the books.

Heather gave herself the gift of a year of intensive employee training. That might not sound like a gift to you. But only when she was confident that every employee could do his or her job as well as she felt it had to be done, and only when she'd trained two employees to train new employees—only then could Heather get out from under her need to do everyone's job.

This meant that for one year—less, actually—Heather had to virtually live at the Blue Cat. Husband grumbled. Kids grumbled. Friends grumbled. Bad Heather. She was leading an unbalanced life. Neglecting her loved ones.

But it was only for a year or less. And Heather was saving herself from drowning. Didn't she deserve to have a business that did well? *Don't you deserve to do well in your life?* Didn't she deserve to have a business that didn't absorb all her time and energy? *Don't you deserve to be able to do your job without it taking so much out of you?*

Well, if one year's investment bought that for Heather, and if one year's investment could buy that for you, isn't it worth it?

Most women know what they need to do to get on top of their lives. The big problem isn't knowing what to do but admitting it. It *is* a problem, because admitting it means doing something about it, and doing something about it means saying *no* to people. But you can see from Heather's story how worthwhile it is to bite the bullet.

"But I don't know how to get on top of my life"

Some women truly don't know what to do to get on top of their lives. Typically, if you fall into this category, you have a sense of feeling burned out, overwhelmed, exhausted. You're putting out too much and not getting enough back all at the same time. You don't feel successful, and you don't feel happy.

The first thing to do is to remember that a tiny little problem can cause a world of painful symptoms. Everything feels wrong, but only one thing is wrong. Trust that you'll find that one thing.

The next thing to do is to find it. Here's the procedure that's worked for most women. There's a kind of 1-2-3 checklist to follow. Start with the first and see if you can solve your problem there. If not, go on to the second, and see if that will do the trick. If not, you'll find your solution in the third item on the checklist. It is important to follow this exact sequence; you'll make things a lot easier for yourself.

1. See if things will be better if you find a way to make your life more satisfying. Sometimes we feel overwhelmed because we're just unhappy. Yeah, maybe work is driving you crazy, for example, but maybe it wouldn't get to you so much if you found a new way to get pleasure from your job. Maybe you run around like a nut at work, and you don't take enough time to socialize with your coworkers. Maybe if you had more friends at work it wouldn't drive you so crazy.

Maybe you need to find satisfaction somewhere else. You can often perform an act of magic. Maybe your teenagers are driving you crazy. You feel overwhelmed. But it may also be that you're coping with them as well as anyone could possibly cope. No one could do better. The way to feel you're getting on top of your life is to find a new source of satisfaction in your life. Resuscitate an old hobby or develop a new interest. That's your special year.

But suppose you decide that no new source of satisfaction will do what's necessary to make you feel you're getting on top of your life.

2. See if you can make things better by becoming more effective. This is a huge area, and you'll have to decide *where* you need to be more effective. Heather had to find a way to delegate. You might have to upgrade your job skills. Learn time management. Just ask yourself this question: "What is one thing I could do that if I did it a lot better it would change things around and I would start feeling I'm on top of my life?" Look for that magic bullet. It usually exists.

But suppose you can't identify one thing to do that would make you more effective and so help you get on top of your life.

3. Make a major life-changing decision. Just think about it. You're overwhelmed by some important part of your life. There's nothing you can do to feel more satisfied. There's nothing you can do to become more effective.

What's left? When you can't *change* your way out of a problem, *decide* your way out of it. Ask yourself: "What big decision can I make that will turn around how I feel about my life? Do I need a new job? A new assignment? A new career? A new place to live? A new life partner?"

I can't tell you what to decide. But I can tell you what to make a decision about. Think big. Imagine yourself moving down the path of life. Imagine that some huge rock is chained to your ankle and the only way you can make progress is by dragging this rock along behind you. That's how your life has been recently, and that's why you don't feel on top of your life.

Now *what's that rock?* Identify the rock that's been holding you back, and *that's* what you've got to make a decision about. Give yourself the gift of a year in which to make that decision.

Patricia. Here was a woman who felt she needed to make a lot of decisions to get on top of her life. The good news was that she knew she needed to make decisions. The bad news (although this is actually very common) is that Patricia thought she was facing a whole raft of decisions. But, again, when you think a lot of things are wrong, you often have to do only one thing to make it better. What was the rock tying Patricia down?

Patricia had been fighting a lot with her husband. She'd been hating where she lived. She complained endlessly about her boss. But she realized that what she needed to make a decision about was money. A lawyer, Patricia had been working in an agency providing legal services to indigent criminals. She actually liked what she did. But the fact that she made less money than almost every other lawyer in America bugged the hell out of her.

Feeling she needed more money was the rock tying Patricia down. She and her husband fought because money was an issue. More money would make their quality of life significantly better. But the decision Patricia realized she had to make was this. Should she go after the big legal bucks once and for all and stop having to suffer and complain? Or should she accept that she was doing what she wanted to do and it paid what it paid and she might as well stop suffering and complaining?

To decide whether to stay or move on to something else, Patricia had to come up with some options for where she might move on to. Maybe somewhere in the vast world of the American legal system there was a job where she could use her skills and help people and make some decent bucks.

That was her gift of a year. Patricia decided to spend a year with all she had on her plate searching for a job like that. If she found it, she'd take it. If it didn't exist, she'd find a way to let go of her sense of deprivation and resentment. At least she'd know she was where she wanted to be. That was a gift worth giving herself. She couldn't lose.

If the best gift you could possibly give yourself for one year is doing something to get on top of your life, then no gift will make you feel better. Don't be afraid that temporarily your life will become unbalanced. Think of it as an investment. As you focus on that one part that needs fixing, in the short run your life will feel less balanced. But in the long run you'll feel more balanced inside, and your life will actually become more balanced.

12

Where's the Rest of Me?

*"How can I devote my special year
to exploring myself or putting the 'me'
back in my life?"*

Self-exploration. Let's indulge ourselves for a moment and collapse in awe at the size of this topic. On some level, every book ever written about people, fiction or nonfiction, makes a contribution toward your journey of self-exploration. Maybe this is the biggest topic of all, ever.

Do you think I'm crazy enough to try to boil this whole topic down into one chapter? I ain't that crazy!

But I do know that self-exploration is something women care about and something women want to devote their special year to.

So I won't pretend to cover this whole topic. I'll zero in on what actual women have done to give themselves the gift of a year of self-exploration. I know that is something we can manage. And I've learned a lot about it from seeing what women have done that works. Because self-exploration is so huge, you can waste a lot of time. It's like exploring a new city. If you just wander around clueless, you might find fabulous treasures, but you might just spend days going up and down boring streets.

What women have done to make self-exploration pay off faster and with greater likelihood of success is to focus in on a simple question: What part of myself that I care about has gone missing and needs to be brought back into my life?

Catching up with Yourself

How does a part of yourself ever turn up missing in the first place? Imagine that You and Your Life are going to take a trip together. You go down to Grand Central Station to take the train to Adulthood. But the station is chaotic. You and Your Life get separated in the crowd. It looks like you'll have to take different trains. Over the heads of the milling throng you shout, "Wait for me." Your Life shouts back, "Catch up to me."

Unfortunately, what with one thing and another, missed connections, the sheer momentum and confusion of events, You and Your Life never do quite catch up. Your Life, of course, gets on the train. But bits of You get lost and scattered across the landscape.

Most women find themselves in this situation to one degree or another. How could we not? We go to work, we take care of our families, and we put ourselves last. No wonder so many women use the gift of a year to turn things around. Instead of wistfully *wishing* they were more connected to themselves and had more of themselves in their lives, they actually *do* something for one year to connect with themselves and put more of themselves in their lives.

It doesn't have to be anything deep to be deeply meaningful to you. It doesn't have to be anything profound to have a profound impact on how you feel about your life. Let me tell you about the Lady and the Loom.

Penny. Sometimes the gift of a year is the result of deliberate planning. Sometimes it just happens, and that's the way it was for Penny. For a long time her husband had been complaining to her about how she wasn't measuring up in one way or another, how she wasn't meeting his needs. She desperately tried to make him happy. Needless to say, her sense of herself grew smaller and smaller.

Finally, one day, he started talking about maybe ending their relationship. As Penny put it, "I don't know, but when he started saying maybe it's over, instead of clutching more the way I'd done, I just thought, screw him, I'm just going to take care of myself. One weekend he went away on a business trip, and I couldn't have been happier to have a whole weekend to myself without the stress of worrying about whether I was making him happy.

"For some reason I remembered my loom up in the attic. I was once a weaver. I'm a computer consultant now, but that's what I loved, weaving these tapestries, and I hadn't touched it in seven years. It's like a piece of me had been sitting up there in the attic getting covered with dust for seven years. So I just went up there, cleaned it up, made some space for it, got some material, and just got back into weaving again. I'm thinking, hey, if he comes home and he wants me, I'm going to be upstairs doing what I want to do. At least one of us will be happy."

Penny's gift to herself lasted a year and then kept on going. Who says you have to stop if what you're doing in your special year keeps working for you? It wasn't about weaving, or about having a hobby. Weaving had already existed for Penny as a part of herself that had missed the train of Her Life. She was reclaiming that lost part of herself. And somehow that gave her the hope she needed to go with her husband to couples counseling and resolve their problems.

Sometimes, like Penny, it just hits you. You suddenly remember this piece of yourself, and *bang*, you go and pick it up. The gap between needing something and giving yourself a special year is instantly bridged. Sometimes, though, the path is a lot murkier, though no less meaningful to you. Maybe all you know is *that* part of you has gone missing. Like when you go on a trip and you know you've forgotten something, but you can't think what. Ann was in this situation; she knew she'd have to explore herself before she could put more of herself back in her life. How can you know what to put back if you don't know what's missing?

Ann. "I'd just been going, going, going. When had I been able to even give myself the luxury of asking myself what I want to do with myself? You know what made this year great? It was that I figured out what I wanted to get out of my life. Not what other people wanted me to want. Not what I thought I should want. But what deep down I wanted in the sense that it resonated with the truth of who I really am."

Ann went into therapy. She was smart, the way she went about it. She knew that what she wanted was to gain a better sense of herself. She didn't want to focus on her childhood but on who she was right now. She didn't want to solve any particular psychological problem. She just wanted to find a safe and enabling place where she'd be guided through a process of self-discovery. She was clear about what she wanted and asked therapists if they understood what she wanted and how they would help her go about it. She kept looking until she found a shrink who "got" what she was trying to do.

When you explore yourself, you've got to be prepared to find stuff you didn't expect to find. That's why they call it "exploration." If all you found was what you expected to find, they'd call it "going to the supermarket" or something. Of course, if you find stuff you don't expect to find, it can be disconcerting. Take it from Ann and from countless women who've gone on a journey of self-exploration. *Don't bother learning new things about yourself if you're not prepared to make changes you didn't expect to make.*

Here's what Ann learned in the course of her special year. First, the context. Ann's father was a musician, her mother a poet. They'd always encouraged her to be creative. This resonated for Ann because she was one of those people who seemed to have a spark or flair that marks them as special. But Ann's life had been marked by a great deal of frustration and disappointment with herself. She kept thinking of herself as an underachiever. Ann learned a truth about herself that was at first disturbing and then incredibly liberating. You can be creative without being talented. You can have a spark of specialness without having anything big to say.

Ann had been teaching art at a community college. For her it had always been the job she'd keep for security until her success as an artist would take her away from it. Naturally she felt bored and disconnected from her job. When she realized that she was pushing herself to be an artist to live up to other people's expectations, suddenly the landscape of her life shifted. Why not just enjoy art? Why not just help other people enjoy art? Focusing on enjoyment somehow healed her relationship with what she expected from herself as a teacher. Teaching art felt more meaningful and satisfying. Ann had caught up with her life.

You can't feel your life belongs to you unless you feel the expectations you have about yourself come from you. You don't have to be an artist or be anyone special to be a worthwhile person. That might not sound like a revelation to you, but to Ann it was the discovery of a lifetime.

Many women have an experience that's the opposite of Ann's. They'd been missing something from their lives, but at the same time they hadn't really expected much from themselves. Still, they smelled the possibility that maybe they had more to offer than their lives up to that moment had revealed. That's why many women use their special year to explore for a talent that their lives had never tapped into. Ann expected too much of herself, and that can be horrible. But Rose was like far too many of us; she'd been living as if she expected too little of herself, and that can be horrible too.

Rose. "I've learned to cope with my life, thank God, but I've paid a price. The price is that the 'me' in my life has really gotten lost. I have this huge backlog of things I've been saying for a long time I want to start doing or at least try. I've lived my life as if I have nothing special to offer. Maybe that's true. But I don't believe it. I'd bet anything that I've got talents or, I don't know, hidden knacks for something. This will be the best year of my life if I discover what it is I have a flair for."

That's what Rose said at the beginning of her special year. Her gift to herself was simple. She would try as many different artistic activities as she could to see what she felt at home with. This was a smart way to approach it. Let's say you take guitar lessons, and it makes you happy to play the guitar and it feels right; that's probably the best quick-and-dirty indicator of where you might have some talent.

There was an arts center near where Rose lived in Chicago. Rose spent her year trying as many things as she could. Music, the visual arts, dance, creative writing. She wasn't interested in exploring *anything* in depth. Rose just wanted to see what clicked for her. It turned out to be sculpture.

It's funny how you know something's right for you. It wasn't as if Rose could instantly turn a lump of clay into a Michelangelo. For Rose the marker was patience. Everything else she tried frustrated her. But there was something about wrapping her hands around a hunk of clay that was both calming and enabling. If she was trying to copy a model's pose or give shape to something in her own mind, the clay seemed to quiet her nervous energy so that she could work for hours without getting bored or frustrated.

They say genius is the infinite capacity for taking pains. Rose probably isn't a genius, but the clay brought out in her a miraculous capacity for taking pains without feeling pain, and that's as close to genius as most of us will get.

Rose had been working as a receptionist. She liked her job, but at the same time it symbolized for her the low expectations she'd had for herself. "There's more to me than this, just spending my life helping people who are going somewhere get to other people who are worth going to." By discovering her talent for sculpture, Rose for the first time showed up for the long-delayed appointment she'd had with her own life.

Who knows where her experiment with sculpture will take Rose? Knowing she's found something that's her own has made her year satisfying for her. Whether it leads to something more or simply exists as the saving grace that makes it all worthwhile, Rose is the winner.

Finding Your Lost Self

It's all about giving yourself possibilities for your gift of a year. Sometimes you yourself are your own best gift. Penny reclaimed some lost part of herself she knew she'd lost. Ann went on a courageous voyage of self-exploration and achieved an important and challenging piece of self-understanding. Rose played her hunch that there was more to her than her life had revealed, and she found she was right.

These are just three of the countless possibilities for finding missing pieces of yourself and putting them back into your life. I'm sure you and your friends can come up with more. My own gift of a year to myself was really a hodgepodge of missing pieces I'd collected. I listed the pieces I'd been neglecting or had long been wanting to do, and I did all of them. Really I was just clearing away a pile of unfinished business.

As for you, ask yourself what you want to do.

+ Do you want to learn about yourself?
+ Do you want to reclaim some lost part of yourself?
+ Is there something you've always wanted to do?
+ Do you feel there's more to you than is on the surface; do you want to find out what that "more" is?
+ Do you have some unfinished business you want to clear up?

There's no single formula for answering these questions. The most important thing is giving yourself permission to take a year for yourself to come up with your answers. As for how you find your answers, maybe you just need time to take the questions seriously. Here are some ways women have spent a year finding out how to put more of themselves into their lives.

Going into therapy. I'm all for therapy. For twenty-five years I've earned my living as a therapist. For the right person at the right time with the right question and the right therapist, therapy can throw open all kinds of doors and turn on all kinds of lights.

But if you want to use therapy to discover yourself, you have to be careful. You've got to be willing to open yourself up to new possibilities. If all you want to do is express your feelings, well, that can be cathartic and it can lead to progress, but by itself it doesn't accomplish more than getting things off your chest. It doesn't take guts to be willing to spill your guts. And a lot of women go into therapy with a hidden agenda. They want to be told, "You're wonderful just the way you are, and if you have problems they're not your fault." This can be comforting, and for some women it can be quite liberating.

But if you're not open to new ways of thinking about yourself and new ways of living your life, maybe you shouldn't bother. Change takes guts.

Here's the best way to think about therapy. Suppose you'd spent years strumming a guitar on your own, picking up a few chords here and there. Unless you were a natural genius at guitar playing, those years would've saddled you with a lot of bad habits. Plus, in spite of all the time you'd put in, there would be amazing new directions you could grow in that would challenge your existing skills.

Now suppose you started taking lessons. What would you want?

A teacher who would tell you how wonderful you were? A teacher who would listen to all your stories about how you taught yourself the guitar? No. Wouldn't you really want a teacher who'd challenge you? Unless there's some uncomfortable stretching of the ligaments and a little sweat, you're not really going anywhere.

So if you're going to go into therapy to explore yourself, get real, get busy, and get out there and find a therapist who will stretch you.

Beware of one thing. Good therapists are enabling. Bad therapists are disabling. And one of the ways bad therapists disable you is by saddling you with a story about how you've been damaged by your past. You have to be careful here. Learning how someone from your past hurt you can make you feel as though suddenly everything makes sense. But if the new you that's revealed is a new you that's crippled, you've not been helped.

To prevent this from happening, spend your first session getting your therapist to talk. The mistake people make is using their first session to spill their guts. You have plenty of time to show who you are, but why bother until you know you're showing who you are to the right person? Spend a hundred bucks or so getting your therapist to talk about how she thinks she can help you and whether she's willing to give you what you're looking for. It's better to waste the cost of one session learning that you've hooked up with the wrong therapist than waste thousands of dollars and a year of your life learning the same thing. It's your time, your life, and your money. Check out what you're buying before you buy it.

And never waste your time with a therapist who's got a hobby horse. By that I mean stay away from someone who has one little theory she applies to every person. If you're different from your friends, then you deserve a therapist who approaches different people in different ways, based on what they need. Therapy gives you the gift of greater flexibility in yourself and in your life. How can you get that gift from someone who doesn't herself have the gift of flexibility?

There are plenty of other things you can do to give yourself the gift of a year that will result in more *you* in your life.

Keeping a journal. The key here is not to spend your time writing down what happens to you every day. That's a diary, and that's fine, but that's not what you need here. A journal is a dialogue. It's self-therapy. It's where you ask yourself tough questions and then give yourself the opportunity to roam and ramble and eventually come up with tough answers.

Working with a career counselor. I would say offhand that a good 20 percent of the time when people think they need a therapist they really need a career counselor. Lots of times, if we're honest with ourselves, we'd admit that's what we're looking for from therapy anyway—a new direction in which to take our work lives. If you're going to end up looking for new career directions as a way to put more you in your life, why not start with a career counselor and save yourself some time?

Doing something new or challenging. Sometimes we try new things to learn more about what life has to offer. I talk about that in the next chapter. But sometimes we try new things to learn more about what *we* have to offer. This is a good option for your gift of a year if you suspect what that misplaced part of yourself is. Why not trust yourself? Why not assume that if, for example, you've been feeling you want to go back to school and get credentials to become a teacher, this feeling is right? Go for it. The worst that will happen is that you'll have an adventure and learn something about yourself that wasn't exactly what you expected to learn. It's still a gift.

Any kind of challenge can teach you about yourself. For example, there's Outward Bound or other wilderness programs. You can also explore the human wilderness. Maybe a new relationship with a kind of person you've never gotten involved with before will teach you some incredible lessons and help you become more yourself.

Going on a retreat. Most of us think of a retreat as being something like a week at a special religious institution. Let's rethink this.

First, a retreat can be any period of time. When it comes to the gift of a year, most of us can't give ourselves the gift of an entire year on retreat. But it can be very doable to take a series of retreats over the course of a year. You might, for example, take four one-week retreats, averaging one every three months.

Second, we typically think of a retreat as a spiritual experience, because it's typically religious institutions that offer retreats. And sure, there's no reason you can't spend time getting spiritual sustenance and at the same time pray and meditate for guidance about who you are and what you need.

But why limit yourself to the concept of a spiritual retreat? What is a retreat anyway? It's a place where you are enabled to eliminate distraction and connect to what's meaningful for you. Who says you can't do that by going to visit your sister? Or going camping? Or walking the streets of New York? Or going to a resort? Ultimately a retreat is about the questions you ask yourself and what you get out of it, not where you go to do it.

I feel strongly about this. We all need a time and place for ourselves where the walls of our usual lives disappear. Sometimes taking yourself out of the hypnotic context of your everyday life is the only way to begin to be able to listen to the still voice within. When you do, listen carefully. Listen for the ways you whisper to yourself, "This is who I really am. This is what I need. This is what I want to do." When you hear new whisperings about these things, your gift of a year has rescued some lost piece of yourself and made it possible for you to put more of the *you* back in your life.

How, exactly, do we listen to ourselves for these glimpses of lost parts of ourselves? Within the silence of a retreat, thoughts and feelings and images come bubbling up. What listening to yourself really means is treating these fragments of the self as clues and carefully following up on them.

Suppose you keep saying to yourself, "I hate my life, I hate my life, I hate my life." You could spend weeks on retreats saying that over and over to yourself. But how can you make progress unless you respect what comes up from the self and then follow it up? *So interview yourself.* Why do you feel you hate your life? What could you do to change things? What you'll find when you interview yourself is that you often give big, dramatic, global answers. "I hate everything. I just want to walk away from everything. I want everything to be different."

Again, just the way you do when you follow up on a clue, use the "one small thing" technique. Ask yourself, "What's one small thing I could do to make things better?" When you give a global answer, ask yourself what that "one small thing" is that would clarify the problem. "One small thing" doesn't give you everything you're looking for at once. But by asking for it, you're following up on clues. And that's how the biggest mysteries get solved.

We never lose the good parts of ourselves we really care about. All the parts of yourself you're wanting to put back in your life are there waiting for you. The pain you feel comes from the way these missing parts of yourself slowly choke from lack of oxygen when they're buried. All you have to do is identify what's really missing. Then make sure you find room for it in your life.

13

Beyond the Blue Horizon

*"How can I devote my special year
to exploring the world?"*

What's the difference between exploring yourself and exploring the world? In certain cases what you do might be the same. Two women take a course in how to write a novel or sign up for an Outward Bound experience. It's the same activity for both women. But their reasons for doing it might be completely different. And different motives open entirely different realms of possibility.

When you're exploring yourself, you're asking what is possible for you. You're seeing if something out there fits with who you really are. When you're exploring the world, you're pushing back the boundaries around you, not the boundaries inside you. A woman who's exploring herself might want to see if she can write a novel. A woman who's exploring the world is pretty sure she can do it, but she needs to give herself that experience.

Now let's make a dream come true.

When You Know Your Dream

We've all spent our lives saying about something, "Well, I'd love to do that but I don't see how I ever could." Now you can. If the gift of a year were designed for anything, it's for reaching out into the world and grabbing something for yourself that you never thought was possible. With a year to plan for it or a year to do it, almost *anything* is possible.

Here's an example.

Olive. "For the past few years I've been doing a lot of reading about Eastern religions. I've just felt they bring a whole new dimension to the religious sense we have in the West. I certainly feel that I've definitely been on a kind of spiritual quest. But you know it's been mostly about reading books and talking to people and going to the occasional lecture. For awhile I've been feeling that I want to do something big to really . . . I don't know what. Give myself a significant experience, maybe. Nail down some answers to some questions I've had. See if I can bring myself to a new level. So I got the idea I could go to India and travel around and meet different holy men and women. I have some names, and I'm sure I can get some more names. I don't think it would be very expensive, but I would certainly want to stay for several months or as long as I needed to."

That was how Olive gave herself the gift of a year. Sure, the trip itself wasn't going to be for a whole year. But planning for it, developing contacts, writing letters, setting up an itinerary—that would take time too. And the whole experience was part of the gift.

It's interesting what Olive focused on as the piece that turned her on the most. Sure, she was hoping for life-changing insights and experiences. But the simple idea that . . . well, here's how Olive put it: "For years I'd been saying this was the kind of thing I wanted to do. But I'd never done anything about it, or thought I could do anything about it. It's just so exciting to know that if I put my mind to it, in one year I can make something like this happen. How can I not do something that I know will make me so happy?"

Isn't that the question we all face? How can we not do something we know will make us so happy? If the only obstacle to doing something so meaningful for you is that you haven't been able to fit it into the little slots you have open in your life, what are your choices? You can limit yourself to those little slots and deprive yourself forever. Or you can take a year more or less and give yourself the gift of a lifetime. It's your choice.

If there's something out there in the world that you've been wanting to taste or try, now is the time. That's what the gift of a year is for. If you don't, you'll never forgive yourself.

When You Don't Know Your Dream

Lots of times our dreams aren't as definite as Olive's. Of course, even Olive had to do a bit of soul-searching, but fairly early on she knew that a spiritual journey to India was what she wanted. Many of us know we want to grab a hunk of something new and special from life, but we're not exactly sure what that is. Well, you don't *have* to know what you're looking for.

You can use your gift of a year to explore the world not because you know what you're looking for but just to open some new windows on what's possible.

Here's an example.

Tina. "You know, sometimes one dream is a stepping-stone to another dream. When I was a little girl I used to go with my mother to the beauty parlor every week. I think that was the one thing my mother and I always did together. It was just an incredibly happy time for me. There were three hairdressers in the shop, and they could do these magical things with my hair. We'd talk about everything you can imagine, and those women seemed so smart and experienced to me. So anyway, that was my dream growing up, to have my own beauty salon.

"Let's face it, it's not hard to become a hairdresser, and if you save up some money and know people in your little town, and have an uncle with some money, it's not hard to open up your own shop. Which I did. I already had customers, and I was young, so the shop was a success. I didn't go for those cute names; I just called it Hair by Tina. I thought that was classy.

"That's when I really started dreaming. Here I am, I thought, twenty-seven, and I own my own successful hairdressing salon. Look at what I've done. I felt good about myself. But, and it was a big *but*, I was stuck in this little town in southern Illinois. I had this strong feeling that I was bigger than my life, like my life was a piece of clothing I'd outgrown. I just knew that I wanted more in my life. I knew that I'd know what I wanted when I saw it. I wanted to see what I could get from life.

"That's when I decided to give myself a gift. I went back and forth, New York, Los Angeles, New York, Los Angeles, and I finally decided, yeah, LA, I'll go there for one year and see what I can make happen.

"You can always get work cutting hair. But I knew I didn't want to go from owning my own shop in Nowheresville to being a hair-cutter in LA. This is my home, and I'm proud of owning a successful business. I didn't want LA unless I could also somehow get a promotion, somehow, whatever that would mean.

"The point was, LA for a year. That was my adventure. That was my shot. See what you can make happen. Shake the tree and see what falls out. I mean, the way I set it up was, I didn't sell my shop. I let this woman run it. We set something up so she'd buy it if I didn't come back. It was a solid deal.

"It was great. It changed my life. I didn't know what would happen. I didn't even know what I wanted to have happen. I got a job pretty quickly cutting hair at this pretty hip place in Hollywood. Hip in the sense that we had a lot of young happening kinds of women as clients. I checked out different things, like doing hair for a movie or TV studio. Other things too.

"But there were two women where I worked, and they talked about opening this full-service place like in Santa Monica but where we'd really emphasize natural products, and a natural look, and everything. They knew that I'd owned my own place, and could really manage things, which they'd never done. Between the three of us, with me putting in the money from selling my shop, and their money, we'd buy a place together, be partners, I'd manage it, and *it happened!* It was unbelievable. My little one-year shot in the dark, and before the year was up I went from owning a small-town beauty parlor to being a partner in this really nice LA place where people come in after yoga class or on their way to an audition . . ."

Tina's story illustrates many things. How you can explore the world without knowing exactly what you're looking for. How you never know what's possible until you try it. How the gift of a year can change your life. The world *is* full of wonderful things.

Pitfalls and Possibilities

In some ways this category, the gift of a year that involves grabbing a little more of what life has to offer, is the easiest to do. The phrase *Just do it* comes to mind. And sometimes it really is that easy. You just have to *decide* to do it. You say, "This will be the year I finally . . ." and then you get started. You'd always wanted to go on stage. This is the year you show up at your local community theater and give yourself the gift of something new in your life. But issues come up for some women for which we need help.

Let's run through some of the biggest ones.

Fears. Let's face it, the safest thing is staying home. Just look at some of the women you've met in this chapter. One went to India by herself. Another left behind everything she knew and went to live in LA. Anything can happen when you do things like this, from being raped or robbed to losing your dignity to simply wasting time. Even if you try out at the local community theater where they take everyone, maybe you'll be terrible. Maybe you'll hate it, and your dream will go down the drain.

We structure our lives so we'll feel safe. You cannot explore the world and the possibilities life has to offer without moving outside the safe neighborhood of your life as it is, without wandering into some new and dangerous neighborhoods where anything can happen. Let's tell it like it is. If it's a real adventure, if it's something really new, there's got to be an element of danger somewhere. Otherwise you're not really trying anything new at all. You're just playing around with the edges of your old life.

If you let fear be a reason not to explore what life has to offer, you will never explore what life has to offer. A little shiver of fear is a necessary price you must pay to give yourself the gift of a year that involves trying something new. Nothing ventured, nothing gained.

If you're not trembling just a little bit, you're not really venturing anything either. Sometimes the best thing you can do is to remember to not be afraid of fear.

Support. "You're going to do *what!?*" The bigger the adventure, the more the people in your life will get shook up by how you're shaking things up. If you have an incredibly demanding job and you want to give yourself the gift of a year in which you focus on learning how to do your job with less stress, that might be very hard for you to do, but it will be very easy for everyone to accept. Maybe no one will even know what you're doing. Take a class? Hey, it gets you out of your boyfriend's hair one night a week.

But just try and do what Olive and Tina did. They both left their families for a significant period of time. Olive for a couple of months and Tina, ultimately, forever. This is an enormous challenge to the people who care about us.

At one point Olive said, "You know how I convinced my husband to let me go to India? He said I was crazy to want to go. 'I'm not kidding,' he said. 'I'm really afraid that your wanting to do something like this means you're crazy.' 'Okay,' I said, 'suppose I really, really were crazy. Like I tried to commit suicide and wouldn't get out of bed and stuff. You'd put me in the best mental hospital, right? If I needed it, I'd get the best. Well, here's something I need. Are you saying you'll do anything for me as long as "anything" is limited to medical treatment? Are you saying that the only way I can really get something I need is if I'm sick?' "

We can't play out the stories of our lives according to the script other people have for us. That script may say we can't get anything we need unless we're sick. But you and I know that a life can be sick even when the mind and body are healthy. And sometimes the only way to heal a life is to give yourself the gift of a year in which you have an adventure where you make a dream come true. So what if you have to fight to win the freedom to give yourself that? Suppose you don't do it. You'll regret it forever.

Besides, love can turn to hate when the bonds of love turn into chains. You owe it to the people you care about to save themselves from being people who put chains around you.

Options and choices. What do you do when you don't know what to do? Most of us are in this situation. We want something new and we have a vague sense of what we're looking for, but we don't know exactly what to do.

The lesson embedded in Olive and Tina's stories is that you don't have to know everything at the beginning. Just act on the basis of what you do know and then learn from what happens. Olive didn't wake up one day deciding to go on a spiritual quest to India. First she started reading on her own, then she took her reading in the direction of what interested her. The more she learned, the more a specific gift of a year presented itself to her. But she was exploring the world for a long time before she decided to go to India.

It was the same with Tina. On some level all Tina did was give herself a sabbatical year in LA. This alone is a once-in-a-lifetime experience for a small-town girl. She didn't need to know more than that about what she was really looking for. She could just as easily have gone there, had a bunch of experiences, come home, and been happy. One step at a time.

You don't have to know everything you're going to do before you go out and explore some option that's been beckoning to you in the world beyond your life as it is.

If there's something you've always wanted to do, when are you going to do it? You have to get up out of your easy chair if you want to check out what the world has to offer. But if you wait, tomorrow has a way of turning into never. And that's sad if there's some long-ignored part of you that for a long time has been needing a special adventure to feel fully alive.

Looking Back over the Four Possibilities

Let's take a look back over the territory we've just covered. I said don't be too quick to decide what you want to do with your gift of a year—unless you're really sure you know—until you've seen what's possible.

Now you've seen a lot of possibilities. I hope you and your friends have generated still more possibilities as you dream and fantasize together about what you might do with your special year.

Here's the key question: *What beckons to you, warm and sweet, like the smell of a cinnamon roll coming out of the oven?* That's all you have to think about in deciding whether to focus on getting yourself some R & R, or doing something to get on top of your life, or exploring yourself and your unfinished business, or exploring the world and doing something you've always wanted to do.

You can't go wrong. The only way to screw this up is to feel overwhelmed by all the possibilities to the point where you can't choose and never give yourself the gift of a year. Well, if the big danger is not choosing, don't worry about making the wrong choice. You can't make the wrong choice if what you choose is an option that's attractive to you. Don't worry if it's the best thing for you to do. Just do it.

Next year is a whole new year. So is the year after.

TRANSLATING
DREAMS
INTO DEEDS

14

Understanding and Accepting Your Needs

"How do I go from a vague to a specific sense of what I need?"

How do you take a need that's as big and vaporous as a cloud, distill it into pure liquid, and fit that liquid into a modest container of one special year? The next three chapters have the answers.

Translating needs into desires. Do you remember when you were a kid and you'd get cranky before you or anyone else realized that you were tired? In a way we never outgrow that. Here we are, highly responsible adults, yet sometimes our needs confuse us instead of pointing us toward a solution. It can be scary to be unhappy and not know why you're unhappy. To be troubled and not know why you're troubled. If the gift of a year is sitting there within arm's reach as a possible way out, then being so baffled is tragic. It's also, fortunately, unnecessary.

As you'll see, the solution to not being able to understand and accept your needs is straightforward. Let me tell you about two women in particular who worked it out.

Gerri and Iris. Gerri knew her problem was that she felt unmotivated. She had been dragging herself through her days, having lost the sense of really caring about her life.

Iris knew her problem was feeling bored. She needed a new horizon, a new interest or goal.

But how could they translate these vague problems into something they could do for a year that would be a gift? For women like Gerri and Iris, and for you, the way to translate a problem into a desire for something specific is by asking *why?* over and over, building a chain that ultimately connects your need with a desire for something that will satisfy it. When you see why you have your need, you'll see what to do about it.

Take Gerri, who'd stopped caring about the things in her life. *Why?* As she thought about why, she realized that she wasn't caring, for example, about work because she wasn't seeing results. Let me explain. She was a psychotherapist who worked for an HMO, and she didn't see that she was having that much impact on her patients. It was all effort, with little to show for it.

Why? "Maybe because I'm not a very good therapist," she tearfully confessed to me. (To get to the end of your chain of *whys* it's important to be totally honest with yourself. The road to true answers lies through hard truths.)

Why? She thought a moment and admitted that she didn't feel up to date on the latest techniques. How could Gerri feel like a good therapist when she knew her knowledge was growing old and stale?

Why? Because she hadn't availed herself of all kinds of professional training opportunities that were not only easily obtained but were encouraged and paid for by her employer. Gerri was growing stale because she wasn't doing things to stay fresh.

Now there was a short, direct chain connecting Gerri's need with a desire for something specific that would satisfy that need. *Needing to care* (Gerri's problem) linked up with *learning new therapeutic techniques* (which turned out to be Gerri's desire). Once she completed the chain, she realized how much she wanted to learn new techniques.

How did she know that's what she really wanted? Because when it jelled in her imagination, it *felt* desirable. It felt as though it would solve her problem. And it was something she could give herself over the course of a year that would change how she felt about her life. It clicked, just the way you can be hungry and suddenly say to yourself *bread and butter!* and know that's just the thing you want to eat.

You can do this too. State your need, no matter how vague it is. Ask yourself *why?* You'll probably get some answers needing further clarification. Gerri needed four *whys* to link her need with a desire for something specific. You might need two or three or seven. If you want, talk this over with a friend and have her ask you *why?* until you identify your real desire.

Let's see how this works in action one more time.

Iris felt bored with her life. It wasn't anything specific. She was just tired of being surrounded by the same old horizons.

Why? Just to challenge yourself, try to come up with what might be an answer to this question if it applied to you. Why might you be feeling bored with your life? Keep asking *why?* and you'll come up with a solution.

For Iris, the answer to the first *why* was that she'd been doing the same work and activities for a long time.

Why? Was she forced into this? No. The answer was that she didn't know what else to do.

Why? Because she hadn't given herself an opportunity to seriously entertain a menu of new possibilities. That was her desire, right there. To play with the possible.

So Iris gave herself the gift of one year of trying a whole bunch of new leisure activities, at least one a month, hopefully more. For example, she would take an adult education course in drawing. She'd join a reading group at her local library. She'd go folk dancing. She'd tutor high school kids. Out of the twelve or twenty things she'd try, only one would have to click. And even if they all fell flat, they would certainly shake up her routine and maybe point her in new directions.

If you don't know what you want to do with your special year, but you do know that something's bugging you, just keep asking yourself *why?* enough times, and you'll identify what to do to put what's bugging you to rest.

"Do I have to do that?" You might be saying, gee, that was sort of easy. Yeah, if it is so easy, why do so many of us get stuck here? It's because we know what's bothering us and on some level we really do know what to do to get what we need, but we find it hard to accept the solution.

It had occurred to Gerri before to take some professional development courses. But in the past whenever she'd taken courses like this, two things had happened. There were people in the class who seemed to have a need to make themselves look smart. Gerri felt they made her look stupid. And the instructors made demands that also made her feel stupid. So she had ruled that option out.

It had occurred to Iris before to go out there and check out what the world had to offer that might alleviate her boredom. But that felt too aimless to her. That was the word she used: "aimless." So she had ruled that option out.

You see my point. We don't know what to do to satisfy our needs because we've foreclosed on the one option that would do the trick.

This is actually good news. It's like when you think you've lost your keys and it turns out that you've just misplaced them somewhere around the house. That makes them a lot easier to find!

So if you're not knowing what to do, try this. Take a second look at some of the ideas you've discarded for what to do to help yourself. If one of those ideas has come up more than once, take a third look at it. Ask yourself why you rejected it. It's probably because there was something you were afraid of. Ask yourself if it really makes sense to be afraid of it.

Do you remember how as a kid a street light would throw the shadow of a tree branch on your bedroom window at night and scare you to death? But when you checked it out it was nothing. It might be the same when it comes to the fears that have prevented you from doing the one activity that would get right to the heart of what's bothering you.

And what is it about some of these perfectly wonderful ideas that's so scary?

Just think about this for a moment. We're smart, you and I. We've set up our lives the best way we can. We've accommodated what we can accommodate. What's missing is what's harder to accommodate.

Something that's particularly hard to accommodate for proud women like us is something that doesn't fit in with our self-image.

Here you are, faced with something that you really want. Sometimes we're not so comfortable when we see what we really want. That's why we reject a possible gift of a year that would be the perfect answer to what we're needing.

There is a way out. Here's what you need to understand. Yes, what you really want is an important truth about yourself. But it may not be *the* truth. It may just be the truth of the moment. It may be the truth of what stands between you and something much more important to you. If, for example, it's late at night and you're tired and all you want to do is go to bed, that's not an eternal truth about you. It's just a truth about you in the moment and about what you need so you can get on with your life. You need to sleep so you can be fully awake the next day.

A lot of the things women do with their gift of a year fall into this category. What they want to fulfill with their year is really a deep *transitional* desire to get them past some stuck point in their lives. Iris needed to spend a period trying a bunch of different things. Yeah, that sounds aimless. But it didn't define Iris. It didn't set up the path she was going to follow for the rest of her life. It was just a much-needed transition from having nothing she cared about to having something she cared about.

There is nothing wrong with your wanting what you want. There's only a problem when you refuse to accept the truth of what you want.

What's the worst that could happen if you told the truth as you actually feel it? That all your answers would point to your wanting to spend the rest of your life sitting in front of the TV flipping back and forth between the game show channel and the home shopping network while eating potato chips?

So what? Most of the things that we need in order to make a transition feel like things we'll need forever. But you'll never get past the transition you need if you don't allow yourself to go through the transition. You know, every couple of years a farmer lets his fields go fallow so the soil can replenish itself. Why should we be any different?

My little secret. I'll tell you a little secret about myself. Once when I was overwhelmed with work about ten years ago, I found a deck of cards in the house. I played a game of solitaire. Then another game. I spent a whole evening playing solitaire. Then I spent both days of an entire weekend doing nothing but play solitaire. My husband thought I'd lost my mind. I can still remember how I felt that playing solitaire was all I wanted to do. I couldn't connect with any desire beyond that.

Why? Who knows? For some stupid reason I needed to do that. And I needed to *let* myself do that. Maybe I just needed to veg out. Maybe I needed to prove that I could do something that I wanted just because I wanted it, even though it made no sense. Maybe I needed to assert my sense that if I'm a worthwhile person, I can do whatever the hell I want, and I don't have to prove my worth with every single thing I do.

The point is this. If I'd been horrified by my desire and fled from it, I would've annihilated some small part of myself. I would've prevented myself from doing something I needed. And I would've given myself the message that I wasn't entitled to want what I wanted.

So if some desire bubbles up in you to do something with your year that makes you ashamed or uncomfortable, think of it like this. Your soul is showing you something you need to do so you can get past it so you can go on to do things that will make you proud of yourself.

If you have a vague sense of what's wrong but you don't know what to do to satisfy your need, you should still feel confident. Be glad you know there's something wrong. Take yourself seriously. Once you find out why you need what you need, you'll see what to do about it. Accept whatever solution is staring you in the face, even if it scares you a little. Don't throw away a good solution because of your fears. Deal with your fears and embrace the solution.

15

You *Can* Get What You Want

"How do I translate what I want into something I can get?"

or some women, knowing what they want immediately gives them a way to know how to get what they want. Wanting a year of dance classes leads immediately to spending a year taking dance classes. No translation necessary.

But some women fall into an interesting category when they think about what to do with their special year. They've got an itch, but they don't know where to scratch. They know exactly what they need, but they don't know what to do to satisfy that need. It's good that they know what they need. But all too often knowing what you need and knowing how to satisfy your need are two very different things.

Maybe you want to give yourself the gift of "getting in shape." But what does that mean exactly?

Maybe you want to find a way to put to rest demons from the past—bad memories, pernicious influences. How do you go about doing that?

Maybe you want to get more money. Or start doing your job better. What exactly do you do about these over the course of a year?

You're actually very lucky if you realize that you have a question

here. Translating a vague desire into specific things you do to satisfy that desire is all-important. You want to avoid what happened
to Lena.

Lena. Lena felt that she'd lost herself in the midst of her busy
life. She was all excited about what she thought would be a special
year for her. She very much wanted to find herself, and that was
how she decided she'd spend it. "That's what I want, to find myself,
and that's what I'm going to do."

But Lena didn't have a clue what that meant. Is finding yourself
going into therapy and learning why you have the problems you have?
Is it working with a career counselor to discover what work suits you?
Is it keeping a journal and just kind of vaguely roaming around the
jungle of the self and keeping a record of what you stumble into?

You see the problem. It's like saying, oh boy, I'm going to have a
really nice weekend, but you don't know what that means so you flit
about wasting half your time with indecision and the other half with
things you don't really care about. That's what Lena did with her
year of finding herself. She spent months interviewing therapists, and
finding more therapists to interview, and then decided that therapy
had nothing to do with finding yourself. She tried meditating—she
figured that would be the direct route—but then she realized that
meditating was extremely difficult for her, so she spent a couple of
months trying to decide whether to seek out a meditation instructor.
Then she went nuts interviewing meditation instructors.

Anyone who's annoyed with themselves because they pissed
away a perfectly good weekend has a glimpse of how crappy Lena
felt at the end of her year.

I'll tell you this. No one ever has to make this mistake. I know
that lots of the things we want from our special year start out vague
and soft. Fine. But none of us has to let that condemn us to wasting
our gift of a year.

Small Is Beautiful

Here's the truth. No matter what you want from your special
year, there are specific, doable, *perfect* things you can do that will

give you what you want. Maybe the room you're sitting in looks a little dull. What can you do to brighten it? Imagine the same room filled with pots of blooming yellow daffodils. Bingo! Perfect. In one stroke, you made the sun come out. It can be the same way when it comes to translating your desire into something specific you can do that will satisfy it.

Why would any of us have trouble with this? We're smart, you and I. When we've got an itch, we can usually figure out how to scratch it. So why would we end up like Lena, stuck with a vague desire we can't bring ourselves to translate into a specific action?

It has to do with fear and sadness. That's right. Some deep, powerful emotions can come into play here. We've all had the experience of the glowing Christmas of our dreams turning into the disappointing Christmas of reality. When you compare what actually happened with what you'd hoped would happen, you're sad, and you're afraid you will be disappointed again.

What do you do? If you're like a lot of us, you say, "Next time I won't have any expectations. I wasn't a winner at turning my dreams into realities, so maybe I just shouldn't play that game at all." When you're controlled by your fear and sadness in this way, here's an example of what can happen when you try to give yourself the gift of a year.

Ellen. Ellen's marriage was, shall we say, winding down. On its last legs. What with work and the emotional strain at home, she needed the gift of a year as much as any of us. What did she really want? To feel better about her body. She was overweight, out of shape, tired a lot, and generally felt lousy much of the time. She loved the idea of making herself the queen of the coming year for the purpose of feeling better about her body. But how? By doing what? To get what?

Ellen had almost as bad a relationship with her body as she did with her husband. Failed diets. Failed exercise programs. So how in the world could she feel better about her body? The *idea* of feeling better about her body was very exciting. But all the specific things she could think of to do to feel better about her body made her feel sad and scared. *Because it felt safer to do nothing, she couldn't think of anything to do.*

It's as if she said, why have Christmas at all if it's not going to be wonderful?

After all, the gift of a year is first and foremost a gift.

The trap Ellen and Lena and other women get into is that they're so afraid of disappointment that they set up huge, ambitious, but vague goals that they hope will inspire them enough to follow through to victory. I'm sure you understand what happens instead. The things these women do out of fear of disappointment create the very disappointing outcomes they are afraid of. They set themselves up for failure, and afterward they trust themselves even less than they did before.

The solution here is to refuse to be stampeded by your own fear of disappointment. That's ultimately what Ellen did. I think in the end she just got tired of doing nothing. Here's what she told me that she told herself.

"If I want to feel good about my body," she said, "the first thing I have to realize is that this is incredibly important to me. I've suffered a lot over this. But I can't let myself be pushed into a scenario where I set myself up for failure. Feeling good about my body is a big deal, and Rome wasn't built in a day. A real gift is disappointment-proof. If I want a guarantee that I feel like my year really has been a gift, then I have to have realistic expectations.

"Why am I so much happier with the stupid little glitter-and-painted-macaroni birthday presents my kids make for me than I am with the expensive presents my husband gives me? Because I don't expect much from them—they're little kids. But I expect what my husband buys me to make up for all that he's never given me.

"I can't have a body like Xena the Warrior Princess in one year. I'll never have a body like that. But if I know women, the actress who plays Xena probably doesn't feel all that good about her body either. So let me treat myself. Let me think of something I can do for one year that will at least take me one simple giant step closer to feeling good about my body. Let it be something I like. And let it be something that gets me off that scary tightrope of worry about failure. A diet? I'll worry about failing. But there's something simple I can do that I know I can't fail at and that will start me on the path toward satisfying my desire to feel good about my body."

Saying this to herself represented a tremendous insight for Ellen.

She realized that she never felt good about her body because she'd never found anything to do with her body that she liked. So she decided to give herself the gift of trying as many different activities as possible to see what she liked best. Yoga? Fencing? Long, slow walks? Pilates? Folk dancing? How could she say which she'd like? But suddenly she had a failure-proof option that would give her what she wanted. Here's how failure proof it was. If by the end of her year she'd tried many different activities and didn't like any of them, she'd permanently cross exercise off her to-do list and never worry about it again.

What does it really mean to put yourself first? It means liking yourself. It means trusting yourself. It means not bossing yourself around, because if you're bossing yourself around, it's the boss, not you, who comes first. It means taking care of yourself, in every sense of the word.

> If you're having trouble translating what you want for your year, just remember to make it specific, definite, doable, and small.

This does *not* mean setting things up so that you're worried, stressed out, and headed for disappointment. Bottom line: small is beautiful.

Back to Lena. Remember Lena, who got so lost in the process of trying to find herself? She took another stab at it. This time she made sure to have realistic expectations and to focus on a specific action that really couldn't fail. Lena was turning thirty-five. She realized that she couldn't remember a lot about why she'd made some of the decisions she'd made. Or even a lot about what some of her experiences in the past had been like. What had college really been like for her and why? She'd had that great job in market research right out of college, and she'd quit it. Why?

Lena decided to write a kind of pint-sized autobiography during her special year. Nothing literary. Nothing to impress anyone. Not for anyone else to read. But just to put down in black and white the story of her life as well as she could remember it. *That* was a real gift.

Would she find herself? Who could say? Would it satisfy her? Who knows in advance? But it felt right to her, and at least she'd have something she could hold in her hand that was filled with the truth. It would be something she could continue, if she wanted. It would be something she could go back into and flesh out if more truths emerged. It would be something she could give her children. At least they'd know her, even if ultimately she didn't completely know herself.

The gift of a year is something almost everyone succeeds with. But in the few cases where women had trouble, the trouble came from inflation. They translated their desire into something inflated to the point of vagueness or gargantuosity. All the women who were successful said, hey, you can't get everything, and that means choosing something, and that means not choosing a whole bunch of other things. So what? You just have to choose something that will take one solid step in the direction of satisfying your desire. Think of it as the beginning of a journey, and think of this as the first step in the right direction. Remember that you have the rest of your life to keep taking steps in that direction and to complete your journey.

16

Making the Impossible Possible

*"No matter what I want, is there a gift of a
year that will make me happy?"*

hat do you do if what you want is the moon? You can't have
the moon! So are you eternally doomed to disappointment?
This is a big fear that comes up for some women when
they think about getting in touch with what they really want for their
special year. They're afraid they're setting themselves up for a frustrating experience because what they're really going to want is something
they can't have. Why get in touch with desires that can't be satisfied?

Well, based on the experience of countless women, I want to
bring you a message about this. *Once you know what you want, you
can always do something so you'll feel happy or content.*

Let's be clear about what I've just said. I'm *not* saying you can always get what you want; I *am* saying that you can always get something that will make you happy. As a middle-aged woman I can
never play for the NBA. But if what I want to do with my special
year pops into my head as "I want a season playing for the NBA," I
can translate that down into something doable and satisfying for
me. If I want to play for the NBA, then I certainly want to play
competitive basketball. So I can learn to play and then find middle-
aged people with whom I can have a good game.

You can always take a desire that's *impossible* to satisfy and translate it into one that's *relatively easy* to satisfy. This is a big lesson women discovered when they gave themselves the gift of a year. Knowing what you want and translating it into something doable is a better route to happiness than denying what you really want because it seems impossible in its purest form.

How do you make your desires doable? You can translate any desire into something that will make you happy if you just ask yourself this question. *Okay, I know what I want—what's one small step I can take that will bring me closer to getting what I want?* The miracle happens when getting a step closer to what you want makes you just about as happy as you thought you'd be if you'd gotten exactly what you thought you wanted. Here's an example.

Francine's story. With three young children, the youngest still in preschool, and a job as a nurse you can't quit because your family needs the money, lots of dreams seem impossible. That's how Francine felt when she first heard about the possibility of the gift of a year. She knew she needed something, badly, but it was hard to imagine what she could get that would satisfy her. She came up to me at the end of a talk I was giving and asked for help with this. Her story is very inspiring, but in fact, what she did women do all the time.

I said, "Begin with your dreams. Don't start with what you can get. That will just make you feel trapped. Start with what you really want. But then if you can't have the whole thing, see if there's some way you can get something like what you really want. Something that will make you feel free and satisfied."

By answering my ten dream-discovering questions and getting in touch with her feelings, Francine realized that what she wanted was . . . Paris. That had always been her dream—to spend a year in Paris. She wanted to learn to speak French, to live on the Left Bank, to meet people, to walk the streets, to see all the famous sights, as well as all the parts of Paris real Parisians experience and to sit on the sidewalk drawing pictures of the people and the street scenes.

That was completely impossible, given the realities of her life.

There was no way she could leave her family and just hang out in Paris for a year or even a month or even any amount of time, as far as Francine could tell.

And yet her dream was still the best possible guide to the gift of a year. I explained that being guided by your dream is the next best thing to living your dream. "Take yourself seriously," I said to Francine. "Do what you can. If you can't spend an actual year in Paris, spend a virtual year in Paris. Get rid of everything but the essentials in your life, tell your husband that this is the year when he's going to have to pick up the slack, and spend every spare minute reading about Paris, taking French lessons, connecting with stuff having to do with Paris on the Internet, maybe get pen pals or Web pals in Paris, learn to cook French food, and maybe, just maybe, plan to give yourself a week in Paris and prepare for it by really learning what there is to do there so you get the most out of your week."

Francine was skeptical, as every woman is when she thinks of compromising on her true desire. Francine said something like what every woman says. "How will I be happy with that when what I want is a real year in the real Paris? Won't I feel more tantalized than satisfied?"

Here's the truth, not the fairy tale: it depends on your personality. In my clinical and research experience, about ten percent of women are primed to experience loss and disappointment no matter what. Whatever happens, the first place they go is to feel what they're not getting. If Francine was one of these women, then a virtual year in Paris *would* be more tantalizing than satisfying. She could never see the glass as other than half empty, no matter how good the wine was in the glass.

But if Francine was one of these women, she'd really have bigger problems than not going to Paris. If you're primed to experience loss as your first reaction, then you have a serious issue to work on.

But I believed, based on my intuition about her, that Francine was in that large majority of women who don't always go to the sense of loss as their first reaction. Most of us are made happy when we get some of what we want, certainly much happier than when we get none of what we want.

We kept in touch, and Francine proved this was the case for her. She announced to all her friends that for one year she was going to immerse herself in the Paris experience. Her friends helped, too. They got little things for her that had a Parisian flavor. They dug up books for her. One friend found an older woman who'd been born in Paris and who'd lived there until she married a GI. She tutored Francine in French. Their lessons were all organized around a map of Paris, and she took Francine on imaginary tours through the streets of the city.

Nine months into this experience Francine was feeling a deep inner glow from all she was getting. She felt close to the city, as if in some previous life she herself had lived there. If only through books and movies and conversations, she had many wonderful experiences and epiphanies.

Then her husband gave her an amazing surprise. It was a week in Paris, just for her. He arranged for her sister to come and stay with their kids. He'd checked with a travel agent, and if she stayed within a budget, they could swing it financially.

Francine's months of immersion paid off. She knew just what she wanted to do and see. She'd developed contacts—people who would invite her to their homes, including relatives of the old lady who'd been tutoring her. Needless to say, it was the trip of a lifetime.

Like every woman who gave herself the gift of a year, the biggest payoff wasn't what Francine actually did. Of course her Parisian year, with a real week in the real Paris, was great. But greater still was an inner sense of triumph and confidence. Like most of us Francine had had the feeling that she was being swept through her life like a cork helplessly being swept down a babbling brook, bobbing and bouncing along. This was the year she took wings and showed she could fly through her life, choosing where to go and what to do. That's the greatest gift of all.

Where there's a will there's a way. How do you do for yourself the kind of thing Francine did? How do you translate the desire for something you can't have into the desire for something you can get as part of your year?

✦ First, and most important, assume that you can do this.

Have the confidence that every impossible dream has its corre-sponding *possible* dream. Tell yourself, "If there's no way I can get what I want, there is a way I can want what I can get, if it's based on what I really want." The confidence that every dream is doable in some way will take you very far.

✦ Next, be creative.

Generate a lot of possibilities for yourself. Write down the first ten or twenty things that pop into your head as slightly more realis-tic versions of your impossible dream. Don't censor. Some of these might still feel impossible. Some might leave you wondering what they have to do with your dream. But somewhere in the list will be some genuine nuggets of gold.

✦ Don't leap into action until you're ready.

Give these nuggets time to transform themselves into something even more doable and more desirable. Talk to friends and get ideas. It was only through talking to her friends that Francine heard about that little old Parisian lady who was more responsible than anyone else for making Francine's year special.

✦ Finally, be open.

Even if you're facing the reality that the gift you can give your-self is very different from the gift you'd dreamed of giving yourself, let your mind and heart be open to the possibility that you'll love what you get. It's like love itself. When we're girls we dream of the perfect man. We marry men who are all too real. Yet love and hap-piness are completely possible for us with these real men we marry, with all their flaws. It's the same with the gift of a year. Everything is possible for a woman with an open mind and heart.

* * *

You don't have to be afraid of your desires. They don't have to set you up for disappointment. When some desire or need isn't being satisfied, we can be in tremendous pain and panic inside. But the intensity of your feelings doesn't mean that it's correspondingly difficult to get satisfaction. It's much simpler than that. The only way to be happy is to know what you want and then do something to make it happen in some way. If you do, your gift of a year will satisfy you.

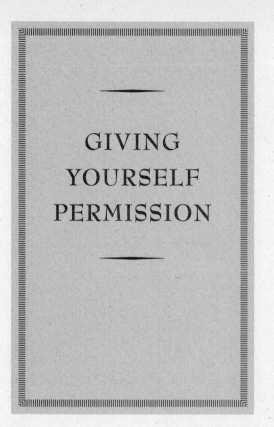

GIVING
YOURSELF
PERMISSION

17

One Thing Every Woman Wants

"Why should I feel absolutely 100 percent entitled to the gift of a year?"

S uppose you see something dazzling and beautiful in a store window, and it's something you've always wanted. It's one thing to feel the happy surge of desire inside of you. And if it's an inexpensive watch, for example, you just buy it. But if what you want is enormously expensive, then it's very different to also feel totally free and guiltless about going in and getting it.

Without the sense of permission it's never possible to do something really big for ourselves.

Janet. Like many women, Janet prided herself on being sensitive and responsible. When her children were babies she couldn't stand to hear them cry. Any mother will go to see what's wrong when her baby starts crying and will do what she can to comfort her baby. But when it's time for the baby to go to sleep and he's been fed and burped and changed and rocked, sometimes you just have to put him down and let him cry himself to sleep. Janet couldn't do this. Every disorganized firing in a synapse of her baby's brain had a claim on Janet's time and attention.

It was like that in every other part of her life. Take right now, for example. Janet has thought of things she'd like to do for herself. Books she'd like to read. Crafts she'd like to get involved with. Has she done them? Well, she's gotten in the habit of watching television with her husband in the evening. And a couple of times when she's gone to the next room to do something she wants to do, her husband has followed her and asked her what's wrong and why she doesn't want to be with him. Get this: the very thought that her husband might take it personally if she left him alone in front of the TV makes Janet feel that she doesn't have permission to do even that.

I asked Janet what any of us might ask her. "Are you saying your husband is holding you prisoner in front of the boob tube?" Of course she denied this. "No one tells me what to do. I can do what I want. It's just that . . ." Janet's voice trailed off. "I don't know. It's hard for me. I always feel I'm going to get such a hard time if I do what I want. I can do it, but I just don't want to go through a hard time to get it."

The grip of obligations. So you see, permission is not such a simple thing. We're free women, you and I. No one tells *us* what to do. Yet the guilty web of obligations has us in its grip. Few of us escape it.

A couple of years ago a friend I'd given a lot of advice to said admiringly, "You never do anything you don't want to, do you?" I guess I'd certainly been talking the talk.

The intended praise sounded good, but I was shocked by the way it made me feel. This woman had seen the attitude I put out and assumed it represented a reality that went right through to my core. And of course she'd been feeling badly because she compared the way she knew she *felt* inside with the way she figured I *was* inside based on the attitude she saw.

All I could think to myself though was, no, I do a lot of things I don't want to do. You'd be surprised at how much trouble I have saying *no* to other people. And sometimes I have even more trouble saying *yes* to myself.

Saying *Yes* to Yourself

A lot of us are in this boat. Every day more and more of us look more and more like women who do whatever the hell we want. I applaud that. But the truth is we feel guilty or scared if we disappoint other people.

On the outside we may look like someone who's free as a bird, but on the inside that bird feels stuck in a cage of commitments and obligations and responsibilities. And the whole time we're just knowing we want to break out. Deep inside we have this vision of things we'd love to do if we could only find a way to break free. Do we feel we have permission to give ourselves the gift of a year? Theoretically we do. In our gut, no way.

Then what happens when a whining child, a guilt-making husband, a demanding boss won't leave you alone? What happens when they pull at your skirts to get you to help them with what they need? *Then* will you be able to win the tug-of-war between your sense of entitlement to do what you want and their ability to pull you away from it? That's *real* entitlement. Not just the kind you feel. The kind that wins battles. How do you get that?

What you need is the sense of permission that comes from knowing what's at stake and why you want what you want. You have to believe that what you want is a big deal. When people start pulling at your skirt, you won't be able to say *no* if all you think you're doing is giving yourself a treat. What you need to do, whatever your special year consists of, is think of it as *saving your life*. Every woman you've met in this book on some level was doing something to save her life when she gave herself the gift of a year. You need to feel that for yourself. Let me explain.

Rocket Fuel

What would it take for you to charge through a crowd, knocking people down left and right? What a rude, dangerous, trouble-making thing to do! Probably the only thing that would make you do that would be to save the life of someone you loved.

It's the most powerful emotional rocket fuel there is—the desire to save someone's life. I've checked, and the story is true about the woman who lifted up one end of a three-thousand-pound car to save the life of her child who was trapped under it. I would like to make sure you have that rocket fuel available for yourself. I want you to believe that your desire to do something meaningful for yourself for one year is as important as saving someone's life. It may in fact *be* the best thing you can do to save your own life. Not literally, but in the sense of saving what's best in you and most truly who you are.

This rocket fuel is your desire to do something meaningful just for you, for the first time in a long time, maybe for the first time ever. Maybe you know what you want. Maybe you just know you want something, and you don't know what yet. But for too long in your list of priorities you've come last, not first. The Bible says, "And the last shall be first." This is your time.

"For once I need to do something for me." This feeling says that for a very long time you haven't come first in your life at all. Your job has come first. Your family. Your friends. Your fears. Your duties. Your guilt.

But not you as you really are. Everyone else's desires have come first, not your desires. Everyone else's needs, not your needs. Other people's dreams, not your own dreams. The momentum of your life sweeps you away with it. Sometimes not doing something meaningful for ourselves becomes a terrible habit.

Only the best. Often it's the best among us who most fall victim to this. Women who give a lot to life are the ones most likely to come last on their list of priorities. Ask any woman who seems from the outside to have the perfect career and the perfect family and she'll tell you that the only way the whole show keeps going is if she relentlessly keeps her eye on the ball and makes sure she takes care of everything that needs taking care of all the time.

What's wrong with this? Duty, responsibility, self-sacrifice—don't these ultimately provide their own rewards? Sometimes. But even wonder drugs have toxic side effects. And sometimes women who are admired for all they have to give are dying inside.

Here are two women just like this, and check out what they say when they let their hair down.

Jackie. "Anyone would look at me and say I've got a great life. And I do. I would never say I don't. My job, my family, my friends— I'm blessed. Part of me feels I'd have to be the most ungrateful person in the world to complain about my life. But you asked me to tell the truth, and the truth is that I feel I'm suffocating in this wonderful life. All these 'blessings' have sucked the oxygen out of the room. It's like I'm running a circus, and it's a great circus, but the show must go on. And in the end, all I am is the ringmaster. When it's all over, no one remembers me. I don't even remember myself.

"For example, I spent three weeks before last Thanksgiving trying to make it the best it's ever been. Sixteen of us, including the kids. Everyone just sort of mechanically said it was great. But you know, I felt invisible the entire time. I'm just the gal who keeps things running smoothly. And come on, let's face it, when your real job is just to keep things running smoothly, you exist for other people as someone to yell at when you screw up. When you don't screw up, they can't appreciate you. Sometimes they don't even see you. But I'm not an appliance. I'm a person. And I want to get something of my own so I get to feel like a person."

Alice. "It's my life—isn't it?—but there's no *me* in my life. Of course I'm very busy, but one night lying in bed thinking about how much I did for others, how much I *thought* about other people and what they needed, I found myself asking a kind of embarrassing question: What's in it for me? Why do I do what I do? That's what I wanted to know—how all these things I was doing were supposed to pay off in giving me something *for* me. Yeah, I go on vacation, but it's like that's a kind of pit stop so I can keep on going, or a kind of bribe so I won't stop the whole show and ask, *Why?*"

It's in these busy, outwardly successful lives that women are most likely to get lost. Sometimes you and I chug along so fast and furiously that we don't realize the degree to which we've left ourselves behind or how wonderful it will be to reconnect with ourselves.

How does it happen that the more your life gets crammed with *stuff*, the more likely you are to feel you don't have a life?

This is important. When you understand how easy it is for us to lose contact with what's best in us, with what keeps us alive emotionally, you'll see why you need the gift of a year to save your life.

The Way We Were

Let me tell you the story of a typical woman of today. Let's call her Eve. That's short for Everywoman. She stands for all of us. Watch how Eve goes from a life full of dreams to a life full of duties, and you'll see why we all end up so desperately needing the gift of a year.

Today Eve, stuck in traffic on her way to work, remembers back to when she was a young girl. How many days she spent—particularly long, lazy afternoons—thinking about what her life would be like when she grew up. She had a pretty decent childhood, but the whole time she was poked and prodded by adults. They seemed to have this standard of how a good girl acts—she's nice, she shares, she smiles, she cooperates, she sits with her legs together, she gets pleasure in helping others, she's neat.

Eve sometimes felt that the life she was being groomed for was a kind of prison—a house of rules and rigid expectations. And Eve felt tremendous pride in her sense of herself as a closet rebel. The rules wouldn't get her. She'd break out. Come into her own. Be true to herself. And so Eve, a semi-rebel, constantly daydreamed about the life that would belong to her once she left her parents' house and all their rules.

Thinking about what it would be like to do what she wanted became a favorite pastime for Eve. All through school, Eve thought about how she was going to live when she was on her own. Just the way you fix up your first apartment so it's the way you want it, Eve looked forward to the day when she'd fix up her life so that it would be filled with the fun and meaningful and interesting things she cared about. The world she lived in as an adult would be a world she created. That was the hope that kept her going.

Not every Eve grows up with her head so filled with dreams. There are tough neighborhoods out there. Some Eves grow up mainly hoping to find a way to survive. But when these Eves do find a way eventually to support themselves, after all that work the thoughts start creeping in: "I've done what I have to do. What about what I want to do?" And then these Eves too start having dreams of a life that's special because it's filled with what they really care about.

What you want is who you are. Suppose you want to get to know the real Eve. What would give you an x-ray into her soul? Speaking for myself, I never feel I'm peering more deeply inside someone's soul than when I get to know the specific dreams and plans a woman has, like those Eve had for how she would make her future her own.

In fact, Eve's dreams for her future and herself grew hand in hand. One defined the other. Who she was and what she wanted for herself were Siamese twins. What's *more* you than your hopes and needs and dreams?

While we're at it, what were the dreams you had for how you'd live when you grew up?

Millions of girls like Eve watched the same shows on television, played with the same dolls, took the same ballet lessons. But the dreams Eve formed for herself out of this raw material made her unique—and your dreams for yourself make you unique.

Let me say this even more strongly. All kinds of strange things happened to shape you as you were growing up. Your parents pushed you. Or they ignored you. Your mother was overinvolved. Or your father was underinvolved. Your older sister was bossy. Or your younger brother was bratty. Your family had too much money. Or not enough money. But none of these things that *happened* to you *are* you. Otherwise you and I would be nothing more than the pretzels fate twisted us into when the dough of the self was still soft.

But we're a lot more. Needs and desires are bubbling up in us all the time that belong to us and to no one else. As life tries to shape us, new needs and desires are stimulated that still belong only to us. Every time you say, "If it were up to me I would . . ." you're revealing a desire that reveals your true self. Certainly all the girls I played with growing up had families like mine. We went to the same kinds of schools. We laughed at the same things. We were tender shoots of the same seeds planted in the same soil. But our dreams for our future lives were enormously different.

That's the miracle of our second birth. Your first birth is when your body is born. The second is when your self is born, formed out of the dreams you make for yourself and your life and your future.

Waking up. Now let's look at what happened to Eve as she entered womanhood. Things changed. Her dreams grew more interesting, more definite, but also more tethered to reality. Having to earn a living started to leave its teeth marks on the dreams she had formed. She was no longer quite as free to think about what she wanted as she'd been before.

But Eve welcomed the excitement, the challenge, the responsibility. The opportunity for power and success. The chance to make a difference. She was an adult now, and she was willing to do what had to be done.

Of course she also wanted love and a family. And pretty soon she realized that to make a relationship and a marriage and a family work she would once more have to submit to the discipline of reality. The wild passionate bird of the self, so ready to fly off and follow its dreams, had to be tamed to survive domestic life.

Bottom line: as a girl, let's say Eve had wanted to live on a ranch with lots of horses, riding all day with the wind in her hair and her husband beside her. As a woman, Eve can't stop thinking about all the work hanging over her at the office, and about what to do when her husband comes home so he won't be so grumpy.

But what else can Eve do? When the soft dreams of the self face the harsh demands of daily life, something has got to give. And faced with the choice between a lonely self, however free to fly, and a self surrounded by love, however nailed down to responsibility . . . well, many of us make the same choice Eve made. We do that because we want to make things work for ourselves in the real world we live in.

But we also make a little bargain with ourselves. "One day," we say, "I'll revisit my dreams and I'll satisfy some of those needs of my own that I've put on hold."

One day. I think you passionately want your *one day* to begin *right now*. If not now, when?

The Way We Are, Temporarily at Least

We're all different, and we all live this story differently. But most of us follow this basic life rhythm of starting out with ourselves first on our list of priorities and ending up where we are today, with ourselves close to last on our list of priorities in life.

But something happens to a self that's so tied down yet still re-members what it's like to dream and to fly free. That part of you refuses to die. It struggles to breathe. When you feel there's not enough *you* in your life, what else can you do but search for some way to put the *you* back in?

It's a simple story, really. All we want is to make a life for our-selves. Innocently we put the pieces together. But the pieces come together to form an all-engulfing whole that sweeps us away. It's like taking a Great Dane for a walk. You don't walk it. It walks you, dragging you along behind. Our lives feel like that too.

Do you need to give yourself permission to do something big for your special year? Just imagine, as an alternative, spending the rest of your life being dragged behind the Great Dane of your over-commitments to others. For five minutes it's cute. Over a lifetime, it destroys what's best in you and what's unique about you. If you don't care about that, it's too bad. Maybe they got you, all those voices working away from the time you were a little girl, trying to convince you that your only needs were to meet other people's needs. But I think you do care. A lot.

The gift of a year has a miraculous impact on your sense that there is a nice big chunk of you in your life. Most women don't be-lieve before their year begins that a mere shift in focus and a slight rearranging of priorities for one short year can have such a big im-pact on their sense of themselves and the way they feel about their lives.

Why not? It's like a Border Collie seeing sheep for the first time. It's like a kitten's first encounter with a paper bag. It's like a first date that starts with coffee and ends with the stirrings of love. When you do something to come home to yourself for the first time in a long time, why wouldn't it have an immediate, overwhelming impact?

You're not asking for much. The last thing you want is to let go of the fundamental cord that ties you to your life. But what every woman wants is the gift of having something of her own. Admit that for once you want to come first in your own life. Then you've just taken a life-saving step. You've acknowledged that you want to do something meaningful just for you. When you feel that and admit that to yourself, you unlock the possi-bility of your getting something wonderful. Now nothing can stop you.

18

Yearning to Breathe Free

"Can I get a doctor's note that says I have to give myself the gift of a year?"

What happens to a woman when she goes for too long without making herself a priority? Unmet needs and unfulfilled desires turn sour. And they turn us sour. A woman falls victim to the *suffocation-of-the-self syndrome*.

There is your self, and it needs to breathe and be free. It needs to come into its own. Then there is your life piled on top of your self, squashing it so that it's not free and not able to breathe. The story of Eve says that we all experience this to some degree. But some of us experience it worse than others. Some of us need help fast. In a moment I'll show you how to diagnose whether you're suffering from the *suffocation-of-the-self syndrome*.

If you are, the gift of a year is an absolute necessity. Don't get me wrong. The gift of a year isn't just for those who need it. Wanting it is a good enough reason all by itself, just because it appeals to you. But if you need it, then you need it, and you'd better know it if you do.

If you are suffering from the *suffocation-of-the-self syndrome*, you're not alone. Far from it. These days a lot of us desperately need the kind of help the gift of a year offers. If there were a lurid headline describing any one of tens of millions of women today it would be:

"Self Suffocates Under Commitment Avalanche."

In a way, we're victims of the very progress we've made. We have so much going for us that our lives are overcrammed with action. We've got so much richness inside us that we can barely tap it. The problem with this is that the momentum of our lives drowns out the parts of the self that most need to be paid attention to.

There are so many ways to lose parts of yourself. In the nineteenth century, for example, middle-class women had more time than women today, but their selves were lost in a desert of low expectations and little opportunity. Today the situation is reversed. Expectations and opportunities for women are at an all-time high. But our selves are at risk of being buried under an avalanche, because we have no time for ourselves.

No one manages time better than today's woman. But we've time-managed ourselves into a situation where the pace of life leaves out the real woman. We're not longing for a way to manage time. We're longing for a way to step outside of time, if only for a period, if only to keep from losing touch altogether with who we are and what we need.

No wonder we feel we're suffocating. We have the sense of having gotten lost in our lives like a child lost on Coney Island on the Fourth of July. Our needs and our sense of ourselves dribble through our fingers.

This is when you're faced with the suffocation of the self. Is your self in danger of suffocating?

Danger Signs

We all experience it a little differently, but if you pulled together a composite of how this *suffocation-of-the-self syndrome* affects the typical woman today, you'd get the following seven symptoms or danger signs. Check off *yes* to each symptom that describes you.

1. *A sense of unrealized potential.* It's amazing how many women look at the routine of their lives and say, "There's more to me than this." Can you almost feel the weight of unrealized potential within you, heavy as a bowling ball in your heart? Do you have a sad, almost grief-stricken sense that there are interesting or important possibilities within you that haven't begun to be tapped? If given half a chance, can you reel off the things you know you'd like to do, like to try, the parts of life where you just know you have something to offer?

Does this describe you? Yes ____. No ____.

2. *Longing for escape.* We don't want to escape forever—there are too many good things in our lives, and too many people we love. But for just a while we want to get as far away as possible so we can create the illusion that we've escaped, the knowledge that we *can* escape. We want to get out of our lives to feel we're not trapped in our lives. Do thoughts of escape keep drifting into your mind? Do you keep imagining, one way or another, walking out the door of your life and hopping on a plane or catching a boat to a whole new life? Do you find yourself plotting fantasy escapes, just like a prisoner in jail?

Does this describe you? Yes ____. No ____.

3. *Anhedonia.* "Are you having fun yet?" Too many women say *no, not really*, and that's anhedonia: a life where you feel cut off from genuine experiences of pleasure. Sure, there are dinners out, movies, parties, vacations, but a surprising number of women today say there used to be an underground river of pleasure running through their lives, but now their access to it is blocked. Do you find you just can't have fun anymore in your life as it is? Do you find yourself longing for a way to bring fun, pleasure, and satisfaction back into your life?

Does this describe you? Yes ____. No ____.

4. *"Something's missing."* Most women today say *yes* if you ask them, "Is there something missing from your life?" What's missing?

It's usually hard for us to say exactly. Sometimes we have to clear away space in our lives to even figure out what's missing, much less actually get it. What about you? Maybe you don't know what it is, but do you have the sense that something essential is missing from your life? Do you have the sense that something significant needs to be brought into your life for you to feel whole and at peace?

Does this describe you? Yes _____. No _____.

5. Loss of identity. You'd be amazed at how many women say the following applies to them: "I don't know who I am anymore." So many shifts have occurred in the tectonic plates of our lives that the bits and pieces don't add up anymore. All we know is that who we once were doesn't fit into our lives as they are now. Take away the roles you play in your life for just a moment—wife, mother, daughter, professional, friend. Take away the worries and distractions that preoccupy you. Do you know who you are beyond all of that? Do you know who the real you is? And is who you really are reflected in your life?

Does this describe you? Yes _____. No _____.

6. Stress. We can cope with being busy. We can cope with having demands made on us. But stress creeps in like a one-armed paper hanger of the soul, where you have more to do than resources to do it with. That's why so many women long for the possibility of clearing the decks so we can get out from under. Do you have the sense that your life is just a little bit too much for you? Do you feel that there's one crucial piece of your life that you have to deal with for you to be able to feel comfortable, safe, and at home?

Does this describe you? Yes _____. No _____.

7. Unfinished business. What happens when your to-do list is larger than your life? What happens when the items on your to-do list stay on there for too long, while at the same time you start feeling that they're more important than what you actually do every day? Millions of women are so top heavy with unfinished business that the guilt is dizzying. Do you have an internal list of things you want to do, need to do, that grows bigger and more important by the day and that you're afraid you'll never get around to? Or is there one big piece of unfinished business that you feel you need to tackle?

Does this describe you? Yes ____. No ____.

Most women have one or two of these symptoms going on at any one time. But if you checked off *yes* to three or more of these symptoms, then you are definitely at risk of being hit hard by the *suffocation-of-the-self* syndrome. The more symptoms you said *yes* to, the more your self needs space to breathe—the more the gift of a year is a necessity for you, not a luxury.

If you're suffering from *suffocation of the self*, there are two things I want to say to you.

First, you can say you have "an excuse from the doctor" to give yourself the gift of a year. You really are at risk. You're at risk psychologically of depression, low self-esteem, anxiety, exhaustion, and rage. And, as you'll see in the next chapter, you're at risk of falling for a variety of false solutions that will make your life far worse.

Second, there's a piece of good news you need to take away for yourself. Yes, *suffocation of the self* puts you at serious risk. That's bad. But what's good news is what this says about who you are deep down. Women with tiny, wispy, squishy little selves don't suffer from *suffocation-of-the-self* syndrome. The symptoms you're experiencing are a sign that your self is fighting back, fighting for its very life. The fact that you're suffering from suffocation of the self means that you have a big, expansive, highly alive self that doesn't respond well to being caged. It's easier to cage a rabbit than a lioness. The same applies to you.

That's why I feel I've written this book for a special kind of woman. How could you not develop all kinds of symptoms? With so much to offer that's been so little tapped into, it's a wonder you haven't exploded.

You're Worth It

With so much to offer that's been so little tapped into, you are the greatest investment in the world. It's not just to save you from damage and getting sick that the gift of a year makes sense. It's for all the positive benefits.

A basic principle of investing is that it doesn't matter how much something costs. All that matters is how much profit you'll make investing in it. Here, you're investing in yourself. For one year out of your adult life nothing, *nothing*, NOTHING is too big. It doesn't matter how many things are rearranged. As long as you don't destroy your life, as long as there's a basic reasonableness to what you're doing, *you are entitled to one year no matter what that year consists of*. You're entitled to take a year off from your career. You're entitled to take a year off from your family even if you have kids, as long as there's someone to pick up the slack. If you are the soil out of which your life springs, you are entitled to do whatever is necessary to keep that soil richly nourished and full of life.

Do you think that what you want is too big? Spread the benefits over a lifetime. One year is not too much if it changes the direction of your life for the better, if it changes the flavor of your life, if it changes how you feel about your life, if it gives you just the memories you need to feel there was something special in your life.

If you still need permission, remember this. Other women by the thousands, just like you, with lives no easier than yours, are grabbing hold of one year. Why shouldn't you have permission to do what they did?

If you have three or more of the suffocation-of-the-self symptoms, you must give yourself the gift of a year if you're ever going to breathe.

19

False Solutions

"Aren't there other things I can do besides the gift of a year that will have the same effect on my well-being?"

T he symptoms that make up the *suffocation-of-the-self syndrome* aren't invisible. They make themselves known. So it would be amazing if women didn't try to do something about it. That's when a lot of women enter a danger zone. There's something about the suffocation of the self that leads women to try false solutions.

It's important that you know what these false solutions are. If you want to feel absolutely, totally, once-and-for-all fully entitled to give yourself the gift of a year, you need to see what these false solutions are that tempt us, and why they don't work. Then all avenues of escape are cut off. Then you *have* to give yourself the gift of a year.

When the Solution Is the Problem

One of the deepest lessons I've learned from all my years of helping people as a therapist is that we can often solve our problems. It's our solutions that devastate us. I'm talking of course about all the false solutions that we so easily and innocently enter into.

I knew a guy who was practically crippled with back pain. The result of a problem? No. The result of a solution. It started with a foot problem. A tender bone in the heel. His body "solved" his foot problem for him by shifting his alignment so that less pressure was put on his heel when he walked. That shift in alignment threw him so out of whack that he was on the verge of back surgery so he could have a normal life again. The little problem was in his foot. The big problem was in the solution the rest of his body came up with to solve the problem in his foot.

We do this kind of thing all the time in our lives. Most women whose souls are crying out for the gift of a year are using some false solution right now and are feeling pain from it.

The habit trap. The most universal false solution is habit. You're free. Amazingly free. It's just that you've been caught up in a routine that's hard to recognize. It's the routines of our lives that constitute the jail we've made for ourselves. A routine, any routine, starts feeling comfortable before long. And anything that feels comfortable feels like home. For most of us this home—our lives—is built out of all the ways we've said *yes* to other people. And who wants to shake things up at home?

But there's some very good news here. Habit is just habit. Just because you walk around in circles doesn't mean your foot is tied to a stake. It's only habit that's kept many of us stuck in the gut feeling that we don't have permission to do something special for ourselves. Part of that is our own habit. We're not used to drawing a line in the sand and saying, "This is my life. I own it. I'll do what I want with it."

Part of that is the habit we've created in others. If you always say *yes* to your kids and your boss and your husband and your mother and your friends, they might possibly be stunned, shocked, and dismayed if you suddenly claim your own turf. I'm sure you know what I'm talking about, but if you have any doubts, try an experiment. Just to see what happens, ask your significant other what he thinks about the possibility that this year, just for a change, the two of you will take separate vacations. Ninety percent of his *no!* will be habit.

But don't make the mistake so many women have made. A habit is not a need. The fact that you've gotten the people in your life used to your being there for them doesn't mean that they can't survive without you. We've worked hard to make ourselves indispensable, but we're not. And thank God for that. Because not being needed by every single person every single minute is our freedom. It's our permission.

That's the challenge: we have to break the habits in ourselves and others that have kept us living as if we don't have permission to do what we want to do with our lives. We've always had that permission. We just need a shot in the arm to break the habits.

Here's one shot in the arm right away.

Do you need to act as though you had permission to deal with some need or desire of yours? Well, just think about what will happen if you don't deal with it. There it is: something you really need, something you've been longing for, a crucial piece of yourself that's drifting out to sea. If you've gotten this far, you can see it, taste it, smell it. What do you think—it will just sort of disappear from your mind and heart?

That's not how the really big back burner issues work. When you ignore them, they don't go away. They just get bigger.

Clearing Away the Mess

To see how we get trapped in false solutions, think of your biggest back-burner issue—what you most need to deal with in your special year—as a messy desk at work. You've been busy, under the gun, so papers and files and clippings and books and magazines and letters have piled up and grown disorganized. Instead of "a place for everything and everything in its place," you've got "no place for anything and nothing in its place." So of course every new scrap that comes your way just gets tossed on the pile. Chaos mounts.

What can you do? You weren't hired to be a desk-cleaner-upper. Last on your list of priorities, your messy desk just gets messier. *That's* what your back-burner issue is like.

Whether it's a messy desk or a big, hot back-burner issue in your life, the same false solutions keep coming up. Let's look at them so you can liberate yourself from what doesn't work.

The reason we get confused is that we have these solutions we think should work but don't. That's the trap with bad solutions.

Like con men, they don't show up reeking of their toxicity. They show up smooth, plausible, attractive. Nothing sells itself better than a false solution.

◆ One false solution: to piddle along, fiddling with the margins of your life—the equivalent of endlessly rearranging the papers on your messy desk.

There you are, needing to do something meaningful in your life to deal with your dreams and needs. What's your solution? You tag along in the rear, picking up crumbs as you go along. You don't get to the heart of the problem. You spend your time complaining to friends, futzing along with a half-hearted diet, reading the occasional book, taking trips, going shopping, looking forward to the next holiday.

We've all done this. But small, not really serious attempts to get what you want or solve a problem are not the same as devoting a chunk of time to focus on it. For example, there's all the difference in the world between taking an occasional bubble bath, which we all do, and giving yourself a whole year to get to know yourself better and put a major stop to running after guys when you don't know yourself, as Jennifer did. And there's all the difference in the world between writing the occasional poem (or making the occasional journal entry, or taking the occasional photograph, or sitting down to the occasional session at the piano) and giving yourself a whole year to create a body of poetry, with all the learning and opportunity for development and cross-pollination that comes with that.

Half-hearted, half-assed stabs at doing what you need to do for yourself don't get the job done. Have you been guilty of this?

◆ The second false solution: to chase after a gimmick.

Too often we run after that one thing to add to our lives that we hope will magically make our real needs go away. Instead of making ourselves a real priority, we try some trick we hope will short-circuit the whole process.

For example, let's say there's no *you* in your life. Your back burner's piling up. You feel lousy. But instead of generating some possibilities, figuring out what you really want, and spending some serious time making it happen, you . . . I don't know, maybe you buy a dog. Yeah, that's it. A dog will be nice. Cute. Something to be busy with. And something to make you forget that you're not really addressing your real needs. Not even one real need. This is the unmet-needs equivalent of the couple whose relationship is in trouble and who decide to have a baby to magically solve their relationship problems. We all know how that false solution usually turns out. Having a baby's great if it's what you truly need and want. Having a baby is an irrelevant, time-wasting, ultimately tragic false solution if what you really need and want is to heal your relationship.

For women who've put themselves last for too long, gimmicky solutions are endless. You might pointlessly change jobs. Get a face-lift. Take swing dance lessons. These may be fine things in themselves, if they're right for you. But gimmicks don't get at the heart of what you need. It's like buying one more organizer to plop on top of the mess that's already on your desk, when what you really need to do is clear out the mess. There's something better and more real you can do when it comes to the unfinished business in your life.

Sometimes it might seem hard to tell the difference between a gimmick and doing something to address a real need or desire. Either could seem like a quirky add-on to your everyday life. The difference is this. We all know the difference between wanting to eat something because the desire to eat it springs from within you and wanting to eat something because you saw an ad for chips on television or because you walked past a pizza place. It works the same way here. What makes something a gimmick is that it always comes from the outside. You get sweet-talked into it. The real solution bubbles up from within you and is specifically designed to deal with what you really need based on who you really are and the life you live.

So if you've got some idea and you want to tell if it's a gimmick or not, just ask yourself where it came from. If it truly came from you, it's probably real. But notice how we fall into a trap here. Sometimes you and I don't have much status in our own eyes. A solution that comes from you? Who the hell are you? A solution that comes from some smart-talking pseudoguru? That's something that sounds like the magic bullet.

Well, turn that around. Trust yourself first. Who knows better what you need, and what will satisfy your need, than you do?

✦ The third false solution: to launch into a messy, even destructive personal revolution.

You know how it is: we go along, and go along, and then we get so fed up we just explode. I don't know any woman who doesn't do this, including myself. It's like dealing with your messy desk by one day sweeping everything off it onto the floor. The grand, futile gesture. Sure, you get everyone's attention. But you don't deal with your back-burner issues in a lasting, meaningful way that pays off in the long run.

Women who employ this kind of false solution have affairs, end good marriages, needlessly change careers, start up relationships that aren't good for them. Some women get swept up into cults or fads. The psychological appeal is that making something huge happen gives the illusion that something real is happening. But huge ain't real. You don't treat a hangnail with a heart operation.

Falling victim to the Big Bang approach can come at any time in your life. When you're stuck in an entry-level job that seems to be going nowhere. When you're stuck at home with two little kids and it feels like the walls are closing in around you. When your career is taking off and you're shooting through the skies like a rocket except that you're going crazy because you never have a minute for yourself.

It's when you're close to snapping that you're most in need of the gift of a year. But this is when it's hardest to feel you can give it to yourself. What you want is in one grand gesture to sweep all the junk of your life onto the floor and start with a clean slate. It *feels* as if only such a total revolution will make any difference. It's almost as if the bigger the change, the more it creates the illusion that you're actually doing something that will work.

But you aren't taking care of yourself when you make a mess.

Most of us have done things like these three false solutions when the needs of the self have made themselves felt. Diddling around, getting distracted by gimmicks, going off the deep end are easy enough to fall into. But just because these solutions are familiar and automatic doesn't mean we should keep using them, because they don't work.

The Right Solution

Knowing what you really need, taking your need seriously, and devoting a chunk of time to it all naturally go hand in hand. One completes the other. Each makes the other real.

When it comes to the messy desk—come on, you know what works. It's only when you do something like take the time to come in on a Saturday, dedicated, focused, committed to doing nothing but finding a place for every scrap on that desk until it's perfectly cleared off—it's only then that you get anything at all accomplished.

It works the same way when it comes to clearing out some space for yourself in your life. We have to do for ourselves what works when it comes to tackling any situation that's terribly important but easy to postpone. Give it time, and make that time a priority. *Make it an issue in your life.*

Prioritization is the key. Did you ever take a vacation where you just stayed home? Do you remember how easy it was to fritter your time away, get nothing special done, and end up with no memories from your vacation? You didn't even come away feeling rested.

You probably resolved that your next vacation would be dedicated to something you cared about. Perhaps going to Europe to spend time in the best museums. Perhaps learning to play golf. Perhaps doing nothing but lying on the beach getting a killer tan. Whatever it was, it had focus. You accomplished something in vacation terms, and that gave you some real memories.

Women do the same kind of thing when they decide to pluck a year from the maelstrom of their lives.

If it should happen that someone is a little inconvenienced by what you do to give yourself the gift of a year, if you should feel a tug of guilt because you're doing something just for you, remember this. You have no alternative. All the false solutions in the world will do nothing but bring your soul closer to the point where it can die of starvation. What could possibly make you feel more of a sense of permission than that?

What holds us back, you and I, isn't our problems. We can overcome our problems. The real demon is the false solutions we use to try to solve our problems. You have issues on your back burner. Decide now—no more false solutions. Take hold of your issue, take it off your back burner, and take the time to deal with it.

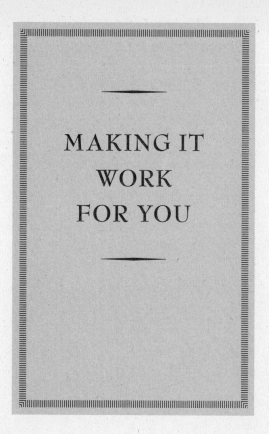

MAKING IT
WORK
FOR YOU

20

Getting Everyone on Board

*"How do I get the support I need to
make my special year happen?"*

The Need for Support

hy would you need support in the first place? Why not just do your special year?

Many women don't need much support. Not every woman is overcommitted to the rafters. Not being in a relationship, not having children, not having a particularly demanding job can all free things up dramatically. And what lots of women want to do with their special year fits easily into their lives. Remember Theresa who just wanted to sit in church every day on her way to or from work?

But here's how many of us fall into the situation where we do need a lot of support.

Most of our lives have fallen into a routine. We seek out that routine. It's the most efficient way to get through the week. Of course there are other people in your life, so you mold your routine to be in sync with others. They mold their routines to be in sync with you.

In other words, we're all interdependent. If you suddenly come along and want to give yourself the gift of a year, that's going to shake things up. There's going to be a little less of you to go around than there was before. You're going to need support from the people in your life, but they're going to be having trouble with your not being there for them as much as you were before.

This is a very solvable problem. Almost every woman who's ever given herself the gift of a year has had to deal with this. Let's learn from each other about the best way to overcome resistance and get the support we need.

Attitude First

Listen to three different women talking about what happened when they tried to give themselves the gift of a year. Since all three were going back to school, they're comparable, but their attitudes are wildly different.

Meg. "I was such an idiot. I knew that going back to school would cost money and would take time from my job and family, but I just started the whole process as if it wouldn't make a difference to anybody. It was like I didn't anticipate how anyone would react to what I was trying to do, not my husband, not my boss, not my kids, not anybody. So then when I got a lot of grief I was unprepared, and it threw me for a loop."

Meg is an example of one kind of mistake: not thinking about the impact your actions will have on people and failing to line up the support you'll need.

Dori. "I just knew everyone was going to give me a really hard time. I mean, already my life was so clearly organized around my having to meet other people's demands. I'd been feeling I was suffocating for a long time, and I blamed the people in my life. So I was already angry with everyone, Bill [her husband], Arthur [her supervisor], everyone, and that was before I had the idea of giving myself a special year.

"Once I finally decided I was going back to school, I had a really bad attitude. I just did it. I was like, hey, if you have a problem with this, you're an asshole. I didn't want to discuss it with anybody. It was like I was daring them to challenge me. But feeling all entitled and everything doesn't mean you don't have to work with the people in your life. If I'd gotten people on board before they got mad at me, I'd have saved myself a lot of grief."

Dori is an example of another kind of mistake: being so aware of problems and pitfalls that you develop an antagonistic, go-it-alone attitude.

Sandy. "I remember asking myself, yeah, what *have* you done for yourself recently? Actually it had been a very long time since I'd done anything for myself. I was very happy and excited at the thought of going back to school, even though I knew it would be hard to fit into my life. The big obstacle was, you know, like for every woman, your work, your family. I knew I'd be making big demands on people. But I just figured that you can't say *yes* to yourself unless you're prepared to deal with the people in your life who will say *no* to you. And I didn't see them as bad or selfish.

"Actually, it's how it is—when your needs make things a little inconvenient even for people who care a lot about you, their first reaction is likely to be *no*. But I never thought this meant they didn't want me to do something wonderful for myself. Why should I think they're out to get me? Just because they have needs too? I just figured I had to help them if I wanted to get the support I needed."

Sandy is an example of a woman who has the *right* attitude going into the gift of a year. You can't pretend everyone's going to strew rose petals in your path. But if you act as though everyone's out to get you, it becomes a self-fulfilling prophecy.

I'll deal with the specific obstacles and the kinds of support you need. But overall the attitude you want to have is Sandy's. Maybe people are a little blinded by their own needs, but they want you to be happy, and they will help you do what you need to be happy if you help them help you.

Believe in other people's good will. That's important. But be realistic. Good will may lie at the core, but what happens when what you want to do with your special year unavoidably has an impact on others? First, they say *no*.

Getting Past *No*

Don't be discouraged. Ninety-nine percent of the time, *no* isn't really the end of the matter, and that's what you have to keep in mind. No one is really slamming a door in your face or declaring war on you. Think of the initial resistance you might run into as a wastepaper basket your kid might overturn in your path if you were playing and chasing him around the house. So what? You jump over it. Maybe all he wanted was to see if you would jump over it.

Still, if people who are important to you are throwing up obstacles, that can be daunting. But I've got good news for you. When people make demands on you and put up roadblocks, it can be a lot easier than you think to get what you want. Every day women across America are giving themselves the gift of a year. They've had to face what you're facing. What they've overcome, you will overcome.

Here's why you shouldn't take *no* too seriously. *No* is the easiest word to say. By the time you're two, you're already an expert. By the time you're an adult you've gained an appreciation of the tremendous benefits that come from saying *no*. When you say *no*, you look tough. You look sophisticated, as if you had wise knowledge of the difficulties of life. You avoid complications. You prevent one more burden from being added to your load.

Now when you come up with an idea for how you want to give yourself the gift of a year and present it to your boyfriend, husband, boss, parents, kids, associates, or whoever needs you in their lives, they might very well say *no*. It's important that you understand the degree to which *no* is an automatic response, not a well-thought-out response, because it means that you have more opportunity than you might think for gaining support from someone you think is resisting you.

You're lucky if you get a direct *no*. At least you see what you're dealing with. What you're more likely to get is a question or an objection that's more difficult to deal with than a *no*.

Jane. She had a simple but very attractive special year she wanted to give herself. Jane had old friends scattered across the country. She was more or less in touch with them by phone or let-ter. But still, when you don't get together physically with someone for five or ten years, the bond between you can get frayed. This is how we lose friends.

So Jane wanted to spend her year taking a trip here and a trip there to eventually hook up with all her old friends. Of course this project wouldn't take 365 days. It would just take a long weekend here, an en-tire week there. In actual time maybe thirty days altogether.

What her husband said went something like this: "You know, I think the kids would really miss you, and now that she's turning thirteen this is a particularly bad time for Ellen. And it's a really bad time for me because you know how much pressure I'm under at work and if I have to pick up the slack from your running around I don't know if I'll be able to cope. And I don't know that we can af-ford this. What with your missing work and the expense of your trips things will be really tight."

Notice how Jane's husband didn't actually say *no*. What he sort of said, in a way, was "Well, if you want to be a bad mother and a bad wife and a bad person, and if you fight for this like a crazed lion, then maybe it's possible."

Ways to say no. That's how the people in our lives sometimes say *no* to us. They make demands. They point to existing demands. Your boss might say, "I don't see how you'll be able to do your job taking off early two days a week, and I don't see why you'd want to with the new assignments coming up."

Your kids might say, "But who will make dinner?" or "Who'll help me with my homework?"

Your mother might say, "You know, dear, I really need you to help me with a lot of little things. And you know, dear, I've seen women do things like this and I've seen it destroy their marriage."

Even your friends. Sometimes they're incredibly supportive, and that's just what you need. But in the guise of being helpful, friends can sometimes raise nagging little objections that get under your skin and ultimately have the effect of saying *no* to you.

Here's a tiny example. A woman wanted to go into therapy. That was her gift of a year. It's not everyone's gift, but this woman had issues she wanted to work on, and this felt like a genuine treat as well as something worthwhile.

A highly recommended therapist had said during their initial contact, "I look forward to our working together. Just take some time to think about what you want to get out of this experience. The clearer you are about what you want to get from it, the more likely you are to be satisfied."

A perfectly reasonable request. But when the woman told her friend about this, the friend said, "Gee, maybe you shouldn't start therapy. Maybe you should wait until you sort through your issues and get really clear about exactly what you want."

This woman's friend had just said *no* to her! She was 100 percent clear that she wanted therapy. So what if she wasn't 100 percent clear about what she wanted from it? All the therapist had done was suggest that she think about that.

So watch out for friends' attempts to be to be helpful. Anything that helps you achieve your goal is great. But anything that deflects you from your goal is a wolf in sheep's clothing.

You see what you're up against. It's tough when people fight you. It can be even tougher when people are seeming to be reasonable.

Okay, now you have a way to identify resistance to you that's attempting to camouflage itself. But whether it's hidden or open, the people who make it hard for you are still making it hard for you. The question is, how do you turn them around? How do you get someone who's standing in your way to stand behind you? It's one thing for your husband to stop complaining when you take time for yourself. It's another thing for him to shoulder more than his share of the childcare.

I will show you how to line up that support. But first, there's something you have to keep in mind: if you have to work a little to get the support you need, it's probably worth it.

Don't fall into the trap some women fall into. It can be a hassle to line up support sometimes. It can feel as though it's easier to go forward without it. But don't fall into the trap of not lining up support just because you're facing a little uphill going. What if you really need practical help and emotional encouragement? If you've failed to line up the support you need, you're doing your special year on a shoestring, without the resources you need.

But remember the attitude that works here. Be positive. Just because people seem to be dragging their feet doesn't mean they can't put their shoulder to the wheel.

What do you do about it?

Turning Resistance into Support

Fortunately, the women who've been down the road you're going down have accumulated a lot of experience dealing with the issue of support. I asked them, "What were the biggest obstacles you ran into from other people, and what were the best ways you found for getting support?"

Here are the four situations where we're most in need of support. We need support from the one person who's most important to us. We need support from our kids. We need money—if that's not a form of support I don't know what is. And we need our workplace to at least permit if not positively support our attempts to give ourselves the year of a lifetime.

Here are the best ways to get support in these situations.

1. "I think you're crazy." There's someone—okay, maybe a couple of someones—who's the most important person in your life. It could be your "significant other." It could be your best friend, or two or three of your best friends. Maybe it's your mother or your sister. What you know is that if this person is totally behind your giving yourself the gift of a year, then you feel you can handle anything. With this person's moral support, other people's lack of support just doesn't matter so much.

Now just think about what you're asking for from this person. You're saying, "I want to do something I've never done before that might make significant demands on you. What I want is for you to embrace this the way I do." This can be a big demand, and sometimes we meet resistance. What kind of resistance might you meet, and how do you turn it into support?

If whatever it is you want to do with your special year takes time away from the person who's most important to you, he or she might feel abandoned. A loved one might say, "Oh, but I'll miss you." Or a loved one might say, "Gee, this isn't a good time in our relationship for you to take all this time for yourself."

Don't think of this person as a selfish naysayer. Instead, think of this as an opportunity for you to explain the real tradeoff here. Your special person isn't losing because you have a special year. Your special person is gaining a happier, richer, more fulfilled you as a result of your getting your gift of a year. The time you're apart isn't a loss but an investment. That's what you have to make clear.

You can say something like, "Do you want to be in a relationship with someone who feels miserable and deprived? Do you want me to think of this relationship as a place where I can't get my needs met? Are we supposed to imprison each other or liberate each other? Do you really want to be on the side of my standing still or do you want to be on the side of my growing?"

Be specific, of course, about how your special year will make a difference to you. Hang in there to answer this person's questions and to repeat your answers over and over if necessary. Answering questions sincerely and repeating your answers is what many women testified is a magic key to ensuring that they get the support they need.

And there's nothing wrong with your promising you'll make it up to him.

Sometimes the person who's most important to you faces a completely different kind of challenge to his or her ability to support you. It's not that he feels abandoned. It's that he feels you're spinning out of his orbit. He doesn't recognize you. This comes up a lot when women give themselves the gift of a year. After all, when you claim some long-neglected piece of yourself or experiment with a brand-new piece of yourself, you're presenting the possibility of a threatening change.

People respond to this fear by saying things that can feel incredibly unsupportive to you. The person who's most important to you might make you doubt yourself by saying something like, "I don't know, I feel uncomfortable with this, it just feels like a weird thing for you to do. How can you want such a thing? I think you're just being a bum [or a crazy person or a selfish bitch, or whatever label this person thinks is most disabling to you]."

Or this person might say, "I thought I knew you, but I don't recognize you anymore."

Here's what you have to avoid saying in response. Avoid being confrontational. Lots of times we have a perverse tendency to say, "Yeah, I'm not sure I recognize myself anymore. Maybe this is a weird thing for me to do. Maybe I am crazy and awful. You'll just have to get used to it."

Having this kind of response might be satisfying in the short run, but what does it get you in the long run? All it does is take someone who's the most important person in your life and make her an ally of your *not* giving yourself the gift of a year. Why would you want to do that?

Sure, maybe part of you wonders why you're doing whatever it is you're doing. Maybe part of you doesn't know where you're going to end up. But you've got to believe in yourself. You don't have to have every bit of your journey nailed down to know that the journey is worthwhile.

Think of it like this. You need this person's support precisely because you're taking a step into the unknown. But to gain that support you have to make it clear that you yourself are not turning into an unknown. "Hey," you've got to say, "it's still me. A new model maybe. With some surprises maybe. But don't worry. I'm not throwing away any of the good parts of who I am."

Then talk about why your special year is important to you. Make what you're doing seem less weird and more responsible. If what you're doing seems like a complete departure, connect the dots so that it's clear how it fits into who you've been all along. You need to spend a year getting a complete rest, for example? You haven't suddenly become weak or lazy. You're the same you, but you're now having to deal with the consequences of the incredible energy you've expended during this past period in your life.

You can always connect the new you to an old you in a way that makes the new you seem less alien. A happy, healthy you who's growing and taking care of herself is someone more worth being with. Never forget that.

* * *

Sometimes the people who are important to us deal with their sense that we're moving out of their orbit by saying something like, "You're not really serious about doing this. This really doesn't matter to you."

This person is saying that you're causing problems for silly reasons. We can be very vulnerable to this line of attack. Maybe you're trying something brand new to you. That's your gift—an experiment. How can you prove that you're serious about something you've never done before?

There's only one answer to this. Stand your ground. Don't get involved in elaborate justifications. You can never really prove that you're serious about something you're not deeply invested in, and you're not deeply invested in something unless you've been doing it, and the gift of a year is something you've not been doing. Not yet. So you just have to keep insisting that this matters without getting caught up in explanations that leave you vulnerable to further attack.

The more you hang tough and insist that you're serious, the more you'll prove that you're serious.

Sometimes the people who are important to us seem intimidating because when we think of telling them what we want to do with our special year we're afraid they'll think badly of us. They'll get angry, disappointed . . . something negative. Julie, for example, wanted to give herself the gift of learning how to play the piano. It was something she'd always wanted. And after asking around she was assured that if she really applied herself for one year she'd be able to make music.

But to do this Julie needed to opt out of a lot of family and household responsibilities. Specifically, during the one hour every evening after dinner she'd be practicing, her kids would have to go to her husband for help with their homework, or her husband would have to go to her kids to make sure they were doing their homework. No one liked this idea. And the fact that Julie would be making a lot of not-so-wonderful noises on the piano during this whole time just made it worse.

If you're going to piss people off, you need a reason that makes sense to you, and you need to remember your reason. It's as simple as that. Okay, people will grumble and snipe. Hopefully you can get them to stop grumbling and sniping, and I'll talk about that when we deal with getting support. But when it comes to giving yourself permission, be able to say in one sentence why doing what you're doing is important to you. Julie would have said, "Playing the piano has been a lifelong dream, and the sooner I start, the sooner I'll have this in my life. I don't want to be an old lady and regret that I never did this."

Just say why you need whatever it is you want for your special year. Why you care about it. It doesn't have to trump every need in the universe. It just has to be something you really want.

When it comes to giving ourselves permission, a lot of us get into trouble because we forget the reason we started in the first place. Make no mistake about it: you will be challenged over and over. The best thing to do is to write down or memorize the reason you're doing it and then repeat that reason in the same words each time you're challenged. That way you convey that you're not going to change what you want to do. Your consistency forces people to accept the validity of your desire.

2. Mommy, mommy. If you've got kids, from toddlers to teenagers, you can get a lot of grief if you want to do something for yourself that takes you away from them. Even for short periods of time. I'm not talking about literally going away for a year. You'd be amazed at how much resistance you can get if you propose taking a night class one evening a week. And you get this resistance in stereophonic sound. Your kids say they'll fall apart without you. Your husband says he can't cope with the kids without you.

And they'll try to stick the knife in. "What kind of a mother are you to . . . ?" "Well why did you have kids in the first place if all you want to do is . . . ?" "Don't you love us?"

You can see right here why it can be tough to say *yes* to yourself when it means saying *no* to others.

But I think we need to look at this more positively. Sometimes, yes, kids can be a constraint. But sometimes—more often than you might think—your kids can be your biggest source of moral support and a wonderful source of practical support.

You have to deal with this on a number of different levels. First of all, if you've got kids, you're just a fool if you announce what you want to do before you've thought about how to deal with the impact on your kids of what you want to do. In other words, the more you have solutions in advance, the more their objections will fall flat.

If, for example, the only reason you're needed to help with homework is that your husband has fobbed the job off on you, then someone to pick up the slack is already there at hand. Just because people are lazy or have fallen into bad habits doesn't mean they're not there as resources.

To take another example, if your kids are getting a little older, they can start doing chores. It's probably time they started doing their share anyway. The fact that you'll be away a little is a good excuse to jumpstart the process.

You'd be amazed at how many women reported an unexpected but wonderful extra benefit from their giving themselves the gift of a year. These women had felt tied down by what they thought was their family's helplessness. *More than half the time helplessness is just laziness and bad habits.* Your kids and your husband *can* and *will* pick up the slack if you let them.

You also should think about lining up help when your being unavailable will be a big deal. For example, if you're away for a weekend or a week, maybe your husband is damn well capable of picking up the slack. But maybe he really isn't. It does wonders for your leverage if you've lined up in advance your mother or your sister or some teenager in the neighborhood to fill in for you. The more you deal with objections and problems in advance, the more empowered you'll be when people start saying *no* to you.

In some ways, the most difficult objection of all when it comes to your kids is your own feeling that no one can replace you if you're not on the scene, whether we're talking about one night a week or even a couple of months at a stretch. You feel like you might just as well be taking a sledgehammer to their fragile psyches.

Not true. Not true. Not true. Okay, sure, there is such a thing as mothers who abandon their children, as there are completely irresponsible mothers. But if you're basically there for your kids, then giving yourself the gift of a year will do nothing bad to them. Let me underline that. *One year of being slightly less available than you normally are will have absolutely no bad effect on them whatsoever.* Five, ten, fifteen years later, there will be nothing messed up about them that anyone can point to and say it was all because their mother gave herself the gift of a year.

If anything, it will do something good for them. Many good things. It will help them become more self-reliant. It will help them develop good relationships with other people in their life, like your husband. It will give them a mother who is happier and who is quite literally more self-possessed. And it will be creating in front of their eyes an image of women as people who have selves and have lives and have both the right and the duty to take care of themselves and fulfill themselves.

Open yourself up to your kids about what you're doing and why you're doing it. The more they understand, the more likely they are to turn into your best cheering section.

During family discussions about this there are four sentences you need to repeat over and over again until everyone gets it.

- "This is something I'm entitled to for me."
- "This is important to me because [say why]."
- "I'm only talking about being away a little bit during this one year."
- "Whenever you need me for something really important, I'll be there."

The more you repeat these and stay on message, the more easily you'll turn their resistance into support.

3. Money, money. Thank goodness some of the very best and most satisfying gifts of a year are free. It didn't cost Jennifer money to take a bubble bath every night. It doesn't cost any money to write in a journal or walk around with a pad making sketches. One woman decided she was going to spend her year monitoring her breathing and making sure she constantly took nice, deep, slow, relaxed breaths. How much money could that have cost?

Another woman's special year is more typical. She found out she had diabetes and was worried about her health. She decided she would gear up to run the Boston marathon. That way she'd both get in shape and demonstrate her commitment to her health. Her special year was an opportunity to get started. Other than the cost of running shoes, it was free. After a year, she'd made enormous progress, but she still had further to go. As happens with many women, what she did during her year slid into becoming a more permanent commitment. By the following year she was ready, and she completed the marathon in less than four hours—great time for a beginner. This was so important to her that she made a special point of calling me to tell me what she'd done.

So don't assume a great year must cost money.

Okay, lots of the things we want do cost money. Going into therapy. Taking a course. Traveling. And some of the things we want cost money because they mean cutting back at work. Earning less costs money just the way spending more does.

There are two issues here. How do you justify the expense? And how do you cope with the expense?

Let's talk about justifying the expense first. Practical hurdles are easier to deal with if you've cleared the psychological hurdles. The psychological hurdle here is feeling you're entitled to incur the cost. Let me help you over that hurdle.

1. You should justify whatever your gift of a year is costing you by making sure you're getting a bargain. It doesn't help your cause to overpay. If you know you've got a bargain, you'll feel that much more entitled, and you'll have taken one step over the psychological hurdle.

2. You should be clear about how what you're getting back makes what you're paying well worthwhile. That course you want to take or that therapist you want to see, they do cost money, but when you add up the total cost, the impact on your life can be and should be so meaningful that the expense is justified. I'm talking about "meaningful" in the sense that it opens doors in your life, gives you new skills, makes a dream come true, resolves a big old nagging problem. Being convinced that the expense is worthwhile takes you one more step over the psychological hurdle.

3. Finally, you should understand the lifelong impact of what

you're doing. The money is an expense for this year. But the benefits will last forever. If you have forty or fifty more years to live, for example, then the right way to think about the expense is to spread it out over forty or fifty years.

Let's say whatever it is you want to do will cost five thousand dollars. For most of us that's a lot of money. But spread out over fifty years, it's just a hundred bucks a year. You're probably not going to give yourself the gift of a year every year. This is a special experience. If it truly is a once-in-a-lifetime experience, then you have to think about spreading out the cost over your whole lifetime. That should take you the last step over this psychological hurdle and make you feel fully entitled to do it.

Then you actually have to come up with the dough. That's the practical hurdle. I'm not going to insult your intelligence. You know how to get more money or make do in the short term with less money. You know about credit cards and home equity loans and things like that. You just have to bite the bullet. If you can justify the expense, then just go get the dough.

But if money is a real issue, let me tell you about some things some women did to get money that are a little out of the ordinary.

There's nothing wrong with asking people you're very close to for a loan. There are three rules about this.

- Don't ask anyone to lend you more money than he or she can easily afford. Asking your sister for a loan of five thousand dollars where five grand is almost as big a deal to her as it is to you is a mistake.
- Don't ask anyone for a loan unless you have a really good relationship with that person. Prickly, troubled, or difficult relationships mean the loan will be trouble whether you get it or not.
- Finally, make sure you set up a schedule for repaying the loan, and then make every payment on time without being asked. Making the other person ask for the money is putting that other person in a terrible position. When borrowing between people destroys the relationship, it's most often because the borrower was lazy or careless about paying back the loan.

And you can go to your parents. Sometimes we hate to do this. But if what you want to do with your special year is really a big deal for you, why not borrow against your inheritance? The way you do this is to say to your parents, "Look, I know you don't have a lot of money, but I know you were planning to leave me something. I would like to ask you for five thousand dollars of that now. Deduct that amount from what you were planning to leave me." In many cases parents don't even have to change their wills. A letter of instruction can take care of the matter.

When it comes to money, more often than not where there's a will, there's a way. All over America today people are hopping on the downshifting movement and finding ways to make do with less. If you live on less in the long run, there's money for your gift of a year in the short run.

4. "Now I'll get fired for sure." Most of us are scared at the thought of taking serious time off from work. It's not just the stark issue of the risk of being fired. You can jeopardize your chances of a promotion or risk losing your seniority. If nothing else, it's possible that people at work will resent you.

You have to have the right level of expectations here. Work is probably the last place you'll find people wildly enthusiastic about your taking a year to focus on getting something for yourself. So you probably can't expect an enormous degree of positive support. But you can expect, or at least set things up so you get, a minimum of resistance.

But women all over the country have dealt with these same concerns and have discovered that there are three approaches to figuring out how to do your special year, given the demands of your job.

First, it's always possible to come up with a new way of doing what you want to do with your special year so that your job is not affected. One woman had always dreamed of writing a novel, but she'd always assumed that she'd have to quit work for a year to do it. That's a serious challenge to anyone's work life. Then this woman went back to the drawing board. What if, she thought, she volunteered for nothing extra at work and tried to write her novel in the evenings and on weekends? She'd also have to cut back on her personal life. But when she did the arithmetic—so and so many pages divided by so and so many Saturdays and Sundays—she realized that she could write the novel just on the weekends, using her weekday evenings to plan and revise.

The point is that it may be more possible than you think to change what it is you want to do or how you think you have to do it.

Second, it's always possible to make a formal arrangement with your employer to give yourself the gift of a year. At the extreme, some companies have a sabbatical program that allows you to take off months or even an entire year without any adverse consequences. You'd actually be surprised at how often positive support happens.

One woman, for example, wanted to do a program the Catholic church set up for spending a year working with poor communities in Latin America. This was a big one: a year away from the job. Her boss was Jewish, but it turned out that he himself contributed to a Jewish program that sponsored similar activities. He was enthusiastic. He not only made it clear that her job and career would be unaffected, he even arranged for her to be on half salary the whole time by connecting her up with a special corporation-sponsored foundation that looked for situations like hers to support.

To take another example of positive support that is sometimes surprisingly available, many women want to use their special year getting some kind of training or education. Here, too, many companies can be very helpful, even when what you're wanting to study isn't job related.

The key is to understand that enlightened employers know that satisfied employees are loyal employees. Realistically you can't expect tons of positive support. But you can often talk to your boss, and if you approach her with a spirit of cooperation, together you can work out a way—for you to come in part time for a while or leave early a couple of days a week or take extra time during your lunch hour. The point is that today there are often flexibilities in the workplace, but you have to look for them and make them happen.

Ultimately everyone's objection has to do with not being ready to swallow the new you. Before, everything was set up to go along smoothly.

Now you're saying there's more to you than there was before, some part of you that your old life cannot accommodate. Ultimately dealing with this involves helping people in your life get used to something new about you and the demands this new you is making. Help the people in your life understand. Help them by coming up with practical solutions to practical problems. Be creative. But don't let the Needy Nellies in your life take your gift away from you.

21

The Wing Nut's Guide to Perfect Planning

*"How do I plan so my special
year is a success?"*

am a wing nut. Are you one too? A wing nut is someone who most of the time is nutty enough to think she can wing it. What's good about it is that when I have to do something—from making a dinner to writing a book—I just throw myself into it wholeheartedly and whatever happens, happens. When I see what I've done, I take it from there. But what's bad about being a wing nut is that I can never be 100 percent sure that I'm going to get done what I need to get done in the time I have.

The way I did my special year reflects the fact that I'm a wing nut. I instinctively knew that if I had to do something that would take a year to be completed properly, I might be setting myself up for trouble. So I just gave myself a bunch of things that I wanted to do that would make my year special, launched into them immediately, and then whatever happened I was okay.

For example, I started taking singing lessons, because that was one of the things on my list. Once I started, I had no further goal than keeping going. I just had to keep learning songs I loved and let the process make me happy.

But what if my goal had been to get to the point where I could pass a tough audition to join a serious choir? How could I have done that in my special year without planning? I never tried to do that. Because I didn't want to? Or because I was such a confirmed wing nut that I didn't want to take on something that would require planning?

I don't know. But I do know two things. First, when you give yourself the gift of a year, it should feel good going through it, and it should feel good at the end of the year. The process should be a pleasure, and the process should take you somewhere you want to get to. Second, sometimes the only way to give yourself the gift of the year you really want is if you do some planning. What if your gift to yourself is to write a book? What if your gift to yourself is to set things up so that during the last month or two of your special year you go on some kind of expedition? What if, in other words, part of your gift to yourself is accomplishing some kind of goal? Planning doesn't come naturally to me. But if I had to choose between a year that required a little planning that I'd remember forever as the best year of my life and a frustrating year I screwed up because it was more important to me not to plan . . . well, which would you choose?

So let's talk about planning. Let me offer you some good news right away. You don't need a *plan* plan, like with diagrams and schedules and stuff. To fit your gift into your year, all you need is a sense of how whatever it is you're doing for yourself will play out over that year. You just need to make sure that at the end of your year you've gotten what you want. All a plan is, ultimately, is your asking yourself, "Where do I want to end up, and what do I need to get there?"

But maybe you're lucky. Maybe you can have it all. A great year without having to plan. Sally did.

When Planning Isn't an Issue

Sally was a transplant in New York. She'd come to the city right out of college to work on Wall Street, and for the past eight years that's all she'd done. She knew nothing of the city outside of a few blocks on the Upper East Side. She'd had a number of medium-length relationships, but most of them left her exhausted. Sally desperately needed "time for me." She found her vision of what would be the perfect gift of a year to be very exciting. She would explore the city, all five boroughs. Every neighborhood, from the bad to the boring. She knew one thing: that the city was filled with pockets containing treasures and adventures—every part of it.

Sally is an example of someone who did not need a plan. She had guidebooks (a somewhat embarrassing possession for someone who actually lived there) and all she wanted to do was follow the impulse of the moment. To wake up on a Sunday morning and say, today I'll go to Harlem. To leave work early one Friday in the summer and say, this Hell's Kitchen I've heard so much about, where the hell is it, and do they have anything good to eat there?

Here's the key. Sally had no need of a plan because without any plan she still couldn't fail. As long as she kept on doing something, she'd be happy. It wasn't as if she was foolishly setting an unrealistic goal for how many new places she'd go see. At the end of her special year she could keep on if she wanted or stop if she'd felt she'd seen enough.

But let's be clear. Sally could get away without planning because she didn't have special needs for how things would turn out. Sometimes, though, we care a lot how things will turn out. If that's true for you, I have a bit of good news. Planning is easier than you might think, even if you're a wing nut.

When Planning Is an Issue

If you've ever had a vacation that included three days in Paris, you know that unless you think carefully about what you want to see and do, you can run around like a nut and still end up leaving the city kicking yourself because you missed all the best stuff.

So when you give yourself the gift of a year, if you've got to complete what you've started in order to feel you've gotten your gift, you need a plan. And if you know you can't complete it unless you work out how much time to allocate to the different parts of it, you need a plan.

You don't need an engineering degree. You just have to answer two simple questions: "Can I go from here to there in the time I have? What are the small steps I need to take so I guarantee success?"

Can I do it?

How do I do it?

That's all planning is.

Monica. Like millions of us, Monica had wanted to lose weight for a long time. But it always worked out the same way. She'd start out "trying." She'd lose some weight. She'd get distracted. She'd gain some back. And in the end she hadn't really accomplished very much. The whole process was a recipe for disappointment.

Then three things happened all at the same time. Monica turned thirty. She ended a five-year relationship. And she started to hear through the grapevine that good things possibly lay in her future at the large PR firm she worked for. Monica decided it was time to give herself the gift of the kind of body she knew she deserved. She owed it to herself. She owed it to her future. Her gift of a year would be the gift of a fabulous body.

But no more proceeding without a plan. Monica knew realistically that if she lost twenty-five pounds, she'd wake up one morning a year from now as happy as a woman can be who's gotten her heart's desire. Okay. One year; twenty-five pounds. Let's say half a pound a week.

Having a plan and being serious about something go hand in hand. Monica went to a nutritionist. "I've got two questions for you," she said to the nutritionist. "Is it realistic to want to lose half a pound a week for a year? And what do I need to do to guarantee that I actually accomplish this?"

Of course the nutritionist was ecstatic. Finally a woman who *wasn't* on a crash diet! Of course she had a plan for Monica. Many plans, in fact, all involving different diets and different combinations of diet and exercise. But each plan would accomplish the half a pound a week. They took the time to consult on the one plan that would be right for Monica, given the realities of her life. Monica had had enough of wing-nut dieting, where you take things as they come and keep falling off the wagon.

Success! Even the pyramids were built by putting one rock on top of another. And Monica lost those twenty-five pounds in easy, bite-size chunks. Dieting is hard. Having a good plan makes it a lot easier.

When my kids were little I used to tell them, "If you fail to plan, you're planning to fail." I guess that was an example of a wing nut saying, don't be like me. They hated my saying that then. Now they quote it back to me as wisdom of their own. Ultimately all of us—Monica, my kids, everyone, even me—realizes the value of planning.

Planning Made Simple

What are the ingredients you need to make a plan? All great plans work backward. Working backward is the *only* ingredient you need to be the world's most successful planner. You start from where you want to end up and work back step-by-step to where you are. It's actually called *backward planning*.

You do it all the time. Your plane leaves at nine o'clock? You have to get to the airport by 8:15 at the latest for check-in and everything. See: you're already backward planning.

How long does it take you to drive to the airport? Factor in traffic and delays. An hour? Okay, that means you have to leave the house by 7:15 A.M. More backward planning.

What time do you have to get up to get out of the house by 7:15? Well, how much time do you need to get out of the house under normal circumstances? How much time will you need to do last-minute packing, put extra food out for the cat, water the plants, and make sure all the doors are locked and the lights are out? If you're honest with yourself, you'll realize that these extra activities add a full hour to the time you need. Holy smoke! Instead of being able to get up at six, you're going to have to get up at five to make that nine o'clock plane.

Notice the ingredients in backward planning.

1. *Realism.* You have to think about what it's actually like to do what it is you're going to do. You can't just say, oh, I'll just get up and go to the airport, and if I rush I'm sure I'll make it on time. You have to think about what's required to do whatever

it is you want to do. Monica couldn't be successful if she thought about her diet without thinking about how she actually lived—the need to eat lunch out every day, for example.

2. *Details*. Really the same as realism, but more so. You need to remind yourself that there are little gritty bits of realistic detail you've got to make sure to include. If you have to feed the cat before you leave for the airport, you have to have enough cat food, and if you suddenly have to run out to the store to buy cat food, hey, you've missed your plane. Any plan can founder because you've forgotten some little detail.

3. *Disaster awareness*. Things will go wrong. Something you expected would go wrong will go wrong, and something you never expected would go wrong will go wrong. You can try to prevent disaster (see "realism" and "details") but ultimately you win by leaving yourself enough time to achieve what you want even with a disaster or two. To make sure you have enough time, you have to pare down your goals. Losing twenty-five pounds in a year is doable even if you're broadsided by the Ben and Jerry–filled sorrow of a relationship breakup. You still have time to make up ground if you fall behind. Needing to lose fifty pounds in a year gives you no margin for error.

It helps to be smart about where specifically you might run into disaster. Just ask yourself this: What's the one, biggest, most likely way my nice little plan will come unglued? You can't prepare for every disaster, but if you have a plan for how to deal with the biggest potential disaster, you'll be fine 80 percent of the time.

Hop on the ladder. Some of us do backward planning easily and automatically. Some of us chronically screw up. And even those of us who manage to get to the airport on time often do so because we've learned the drill. Give us something to do that we've never done before and we're at risk of screwing up again.

The easiest way to plan your special year, if planning is necessary for success, is to use the ladder technique. Imagine a ladder with twelve steps, one for each month. There you are at the bottom, fueled by hope. There you are at the top, arms raised in triumph.

Now go ahead and draw a ladder on a piece of paper with twelve steps, with little stick figures of a triumphant you at the top and a hopeful you at the bottom. What are you needing to do during the last step, just before you reach your goal? What about the step before that? The step before that?

Work your way down like this to the first step. You've just forced yourself to do backward planning in twelve steps. Now challenge yourself. Is this realistic? Can you do it in the time you have available? Have you given yourself enough time at the beginning to lay the foundation? Have you given yourself enough time at the end to tie up loose ends and put all the finishing touches on?

For Monica, of course, using the ladder technique was incredibly easy. She just wrote in "two pounds" at each of the twelve steps of her weight-loss ladder (half a pound a week). She already knew from the nutritionist that this was doable, and how to do it.

But let's not kid ourselves. Some of the things we need to do to give ourselves a special year require us to put more work into the planning.

Jodie's Story

Jodie had been a film major in college, but like most film majors she had gone on to do something else after graduation. For the past several years she had been working writing software for a major computer software developer. Let's just say that her work wasn't as exciting as it might sound, and it might not even sound all that exciting. Of course Jodie's dreams of making movies had never died. They only got dimmer as work and family responsibilities piled up. And as her dreams had gotten dimmer, Jodie's sense that a vital part of herself was dying had grown stronger.

She knew that at some point she'd just have to make some kind of movie. Jodie came from a large Jewish family. On her father's side were Jews who had lived in America for over a hundred years, starting small businesses in small southern towns. Her mother's father had fled Nazi Germany before the Holocaust, as had most of his relatives, and her mother's mother had been a Holocaust survivor along with a sister and a couple of cousins. Put together, both sides of her family gave an entire spectrum of the Jewish experience in America. Old-timers and newcomers.

Jodie wanted to make a movie that would capture the meaning and drama and personal dimension of this experience for people of her generation before it was too late and the people who could tell their stories were dead.

You can immediately sense that this desire screams out the need for smart planning, if the dream isn't to turn into a disaster. Here are some of the things Jodie did to make sure the planning was successful and that she got the gift this year was designed to give her.

She was a smart woman. She wrote in her notebook, "I can't guarantee my little movie will be wonderful. But if I use my head, I can guarantee, damn it, that I will make my little movie."

Jodie did what many of us need to do. After she told her boss what she wanted to do, she asked him if he'd put her on a part-time schedule for one year. She asked her husband to take over more than his share of household responsibilities. Her boss and her husband said *yes*.

♦ What This Means for You. ♦

You can't put a size nine foot into a size seven shoe. Something's got to give. If whatever it is you want to do in your special year is going to need a lot of time, then you have to do something to give yourself more time. It usually requires radical surgery to fit a size nine foot into a size seven shoe, but if you've got to do it, you've got to do it. Don't *not* do it and then at the end of your year complain that you couldn't do everything you wanted to do.

Jodie also looked realistically at what she could accomplish with her movie. She had no budget, and she'd never made a movie before. So she cut all the fat out of her ambitions. She'd make the movie with a video camera, not a movie camera. She'd stay away from anything that required special effects. No jazzy editing. She said to me as she was getting started, "Look, this is a simple story of people talking about their lives to show the differences and similarities among these lives. All I have to do is shoot footage of people talking about events in their lives they're longing to talk about and I'll get what I need."

◆ What This Means for You. ◆

It's better to succeed at something small than fail at something big. Whenever planning is involved, scale down. Even if you don't think you need to scale down, scale down. Even if you think you'll betray the spirit of what it is you want to do if you scale down, scale down anyway. How can I say this so confidently? Because when I've talked to women who ran into trouble giving themselves a special year, trying to do too much was a theme that came up over and over. If you're not sure whether what you're trying to do is too much or not, talk to someone with experience. The nutritionist told Monica that twenty-five pounds in a year was highly doable. The filmmakers Jodie talked to all said that the only way she could do her film would be if she pared it down to the minimum.

Here's another thing Jodie did. Being aware of the steps in her ladder, Jodie asked herself where she might run into a time crunch. She thought, "Setting up a video camera and letting it run while people talk is the easiest thing in the world. I know I'm going to get miles of footage once I get people to talk. After all, they're my family. But editing all this footage could be a real bitch and take a lot of time. Plus one more thing. The people in my family are living all over the place, and they've all got plans of their own. Setting up these tapings could be a real bitch too."

Jodie realized where she could get bogged down on the road to getting what she wanted. So she didn't take for granted that it would be easy to set up tapings. She pushed to make a lot of it happen fast.

Knowing that the editing would take a lot of time, she made sure to finish shooting five months into her year. That's right. Five months. Leaving seven months for editing. Because she said to herself, "I'm sure I can do the editing in five months. At the most. But since this is the sticky part, I'd better give myself another two months over and above that just to be on the safe side."

♦ What This Means for You. ♦

Every plan, no matter what, has a soft underbelly of vulnerability somewhere. You're in the middle of making dinner and you're missing an ingredient so you have to run to the supermarket. Round trip door-to-door, it shouldn't take you more than thirty-five minutes. Except for one thing. You always run into somebody and they always want to talk and you always have trouble pulling yourself away. So your plan for shopping in thirty-five minutes depends on not running into people or in being prepared to say you don't have time to talk. So you've got to choose. Shop, talk, and ruin dinner. Or shop, be prepared to make someone mad at you, and have the dinner come out right. Being aware of the way every plan is vulnerable like this will save your butt, just the way it did for Jodie. You've got to challenge yourself. Not "what could go wrong?" but "how will things go wrong?" Only when you see where the parts of your plan lend themselves to trouble can you change your plan to allow for that trouble.

Even Monica had to do this with her simple half-a-pound-a-week plan. Like trolls under a bridge, holidays lurked within her plan. Christmas, Thanksgiving, birthday celebrations, anniversary dinners. How do you lose half a pound during a week that contains Thanksgiving, for example?

By planning for it.

Planning's actually easy, particularly when you work backward from where you want to end up. If you can plan to get to the airport on time, then you can plan anything.

Inside the Mind of a Wing Nut

Why do some women have trouble with planning sometimes? Because they're stupid? Lazy? Neurotic?

None of these. I know this because every woman I've ever met who has complained about having trouble making plans has some activity in her life requiring planning that she's very good at. So something else is going on.

I want to make sure that you set yourself up for success when it comes to giving yourself the gift of a year. So here's how to *avoid* setting yourself up for failure when it comes to planning.

◆ Sometimes planning fails because you've said, "Oh, I'm just not one of those people who make plans."

Sometimes we're not *just* wing nuts. We're *proud* wing nuts. This can be a real woman's issue. Women are soft, intuitive, emotionally oriented, leading with our hearts. At least this is one vision of women. And it's an antiplanning vision. Sometimes it can seem as though we have a word for a woman with a plan: bitch. That's because having a plan makes it harder to be nice, and if a woman is not nice, she's a bitch.

Nowadays we know this isn't true. Women are natural planners. Because we're the ones who give birth to and care for infants, nature designed us to be planners. If you add the fact that today women are educated and out there in the world doing everything men do, that makes us great planners.

Let me put it like this. If Napoleon had been a woman, he wouldn't have invaded Russia with all that cold weather and so far from access to food.

Why *else* would a woman say "I'm not one of these planning people"? Maybe because she sees herself as somehow "creative," "artistic." As if planning is the antithesis of beauty and wonder. Well, of

course there's an element of intuition and spontaneity in most creative endeavors, and most of the things you and I do require cre-
ativity. But the most important truth about creative people is that
they produce. Emily Dickinson, Jane Austen, Mary Cassatt, Virginia
Woolf, Iris Murdoch, Cindy Sherman, Madonna—all these women
were and are people who get the job done.

To get the job done, you have to know what you're doing. And
what *is* knowing what you're doing, other than going by some kind
of plan, some inner road map that tells you where you are and helps
you get to where you want to go?

Too often "I'm not one of those planning people" is just a way of
saying, "I don't want to be someone who actually does anything."
We're afraid. We're like inner agoraphobics. Instead of actually being afraid to go out in the world, we go outside physically but we're
afraid to take anything on we really care about out there in the
world.

• Sometimes planning fails because you're scared of failure.

What if, for example, you spend your year training to run a marathon, but you never really progress to the point where you won't
embarrass yourself? Some dreams come with a real risk of failure.
How can you give yourself permission to want something like that?

Let's be realistic. If what you are trying to do is pretty much
doomed to failure, then maybe you should focus on doing something else. But you don't need a guarantee of success for your special
year to make sense.

Here's a rule of thumb. If you think there's a fifty/fifty chance of
success or better, then go for it.

Of course, fifty/fifty is just a rough guide. If you're spending a lot
of money, then you need to make sure that the odds of success are
much better than fifty/fifty. On the other hand, if you're going to get
a lot out of the experience no matter what happens—let's say you
devote your special year to running for town council—then the experience can be worthwhile even if your chance of success is small.

Talk to people whose whole life is behind them. Ask them where
their regrets lie. Failures? Not as much as you might think.

The biggest regrets lie in the things these people wanted to do, thought of doing, flirted with doing, but never actually did.

Bottom line: be afraid of being stupid, be afraid of missing out on great experiences, but don't be afraid of failure. Planning prevents failure. Don't let fear of failure prevent planning.

✦ Sometimes planning fails because we don't really want what we're planning for.

Jodie had to face this. She'd dreamed of being a filmmaker. Then real life took over. Then suddenly she had this opportunity to make a movie. *What if it was crap?* There was real danger of that. Sometimes you can work hard to make a movie and nothing jells. The dream movies you'd imagined making were wonderful. Now there's this real movie, and it betrays you and your dreams.

But there is a way out. *Don't plan.* Just sort of throw it together. Let it all be a kind of spontaneous happening. Then if it all falls apart, your fingerprints aren't on it. What do you expect from one of these fun, random, slapped-together things?

You see the benefit of not planning? It takes you off the hook.

Another benefit is that by not planning you don't impose your needs on anyone and no one's mad at you. Jodie had to make people mad at her to get her film done. She had to shout at her sweet, old grandmother to get her to stop putting off being filmed because she was afraid she looked old. "You're eighty-one, grandma! Everyone knows how old you are. You'd look weird if you looked anything other than the way you look. You're beautiful. You should be proud."

Of course her grandmother said, "If you're going to yell at me, then for sure I'm not going to let you make a movie about me. I'm going to tell everybody else not to be in the movie of an ungrateful little girl who yells at her grandmother." But her grandmother was secretly proud and pleased.

There were many fights. Jodie had fights with her husband during the last couple of months. Just when she most needed time to finish up the editing he was starting to get sick of how much time her moviemaking took from their lives together.

Better not to have a plan. Then you don't fight. Of course you don't get your movie either. But everyone likes you.

Do you buy that? Of course not. And you're right not to buy that. Here's what happened with Jodie. She had fights with her family, and people got mad at her, but she kept to her plan and made her movie. She made up with the people she had fights with. That was easy because they weren't crazy people and what she was doing was basically good. And they understood what she was doing. So what if people fight? If they basically have good intentions, they make up.

And Jodie had made a great movie by the end. Maybe not an Academy Award winner. But it was a movie-length video that was moving and meaningful for everyone involved. It got shown around town a lot. And it was aired by the local public television station.

The gift Jodie gave herself turned into a gift for others. Most of the gifts you and I need don't turn into gifts for others in such an obvious, direct way. Nonetheless, if planning is required, you'd better plan or else just come out and say you don't want your own gift. The truth is that for all our fears and doubts, planning is a small price to pay to get an enormous gift.

Remember: all planning is backward planning. Start from where you want to end up, and fill in the missing steps. If a squirrel can plan its nuts, you're nuts not to plan.

22

Finding Time

*"How do I get enough time every day
to do my special year?"*

Think of the absolutely busiest woman you know of, the busiest woman you can imagine. She might be a professional or an executive with a mind-blowing schedule. She might be a mother with a full-time job, a part-time job, small kids, a house, a husband, a mother—a whole raft of responsibilities. We all know women like this. In my clinical work and research I've seen the insides of countless women's lives, and I know that most of us *are* women like this, or at least come close.

We know about being busy, you and I.

So there are no illusions here when I say there isn't a woman in the world who can't find the time to give herself the gift of a year. You can always clear away some time for yourself to give yourself a year you need, a year you'll always remember. I'm not saying you can keep doing your job as a hospital administrator and go on a year-long archaeological expedition at the same time. You can't be unrealistic. But I don't think you'd be that unrealistic anyway.

The danger most women face today isn't unrealistically thinking they have more time than they really do. A bigger danger more women face is unrealistically thinking that they don't have the time they need to do something special for themselves. We think of a special year we need and want that's close to being doable, but then out of a false sense of realism we just say we can't do it.

The best kind of realism doesn't go around pointing to all the things that are impossible. The best kind of realism looks for what just might be possible given what you really want and then says, "Let's see if we can find a way to make it happen."

So in that spirit of optimistic realism, let's learn from the masters. These are women who've fought in the same time trenches you and I are struggling in and who've found ways to get more time for themselves. These are women who discovered what works to free up an entire year as well was what works to free up five-minute chunks of time throughout the day.

You should always be optimistic that you can find more time somewhere. And you need that optimism. Because of the lives we lead and, I think, because we're women, people will try to make claims on our time. We sometimes find it hard to resist these claims. Before you know it you can get that tight feeling in your chest that signals an attack on your special year, on your freedom, on your very self. But if you keep staying true to the belief that you can always get time for yourself, you can preserve the sanctity of your special year.

This kind of optimism is realistic. All the women here found ways to get time for themselves even though they were living lives very much like yours. Different women's ideas for how to find more time, of course, apply to different contexts. Not every idea will fit your life. But if you take away just one idea that works for you from all these women, that will give you all the time you need for your special year.

The Ten Best Ideas for Getting More Time

Zoe. "*I spent a lot of time worrying about how I was going to have to struggle with everyone to get more time for myself. In the end though, I took the time I needed without telling anyone. Everyone just thought I was busy. My advice is don't ask. Just do it.*"

You have to know what you're doing, of course, but this strategy can be amazingly freeing. I see this everywhere. People will say *no* if you ask. People won't say anything if you just do it. The key here is not being greedy. This idea works best for women who need an extra hour or two here and there. If you need more than that and try this idea, you might get busted.

♦ Time-finding Tip #1 ♦

Don't ask for time for yourself, just take it. If you ask, people can say *no*. If you just do it, then you've done it and you've got it. Your being happy is the only change they'll notice.

Drew. *"If you make a really big fuss about it, maybe you'll get it. I remember I once asked my boss if I could leave work an hour early to pick up my kid sister at the airport. He went crazy. He didn't care that it was her first visit to the big city. He was just, like, you don't take off from work to have social engagements. Then I had to have a chest x-ray because I'd been coughing. How long does it take to x-ray your chest? Two seconds? But he gave me the whole day off. I remembered that when I decided to give myself the gift of a year. Yeah, I lied and made up this whole big family emergency with my mother getting Alzheimer's, but it worked to get him off my back."*

Okay, lying is wrong, but the point is that the more important you can make your special year seem, the more likely you are to convince people to give you time for it. Let's say you decide you want to give yourself a year to get into good physical shape. Do you tell people it's so you'll look good on the beach? Or do you say it's for your health? You get the point.

When Jodie wanted to make her film, she didn't tell her boss it was important because "it was something I always wanted to do." That kind of thing is valid for you and me, but not for bosses. She told her boss it was important because it was part of documenting the Holocaust and that her aging relatives were dying off.

♦ **Time-finding Tip #2** ♦

The more you can dramatize and magnify why you need time for yourself, the more likely you are to get it. People will take your needs as seriously as you appear to take them.

Robin. *"My problem wasn't my boss. I'm a doctor, and where I work I'm really responsible for my own time. My problem was that I'd start saying yes to a whole bunch of people and the next thing you'd know I'd used up all the time I needed for myself. That's why I failed the first time I tried to give myself the gift of a year. I never showed up for my art classes. What I finally did that worked was write down in my appointment book as far in advance as possible the times I needed for myself. I put down the word triage in my book, because that's where you sort out who needs help the most, and that was me. I can't tell you how important it was to me to treat that time as sacred. It wasn't just that I needed the gift of a year to feel I could breathe. I needed to prove to myself that I could take care of myself, that I would show up for myself."*

One of the reasons many women have trouble finding time for themselves isn't that they're overcommitted. They're underprioritized. They're willing to give themselves the gift of a year, but they'll only make time for themselves when everyone else's needs are satisfied. It's hard to say *no* to people. But for some reason when you've written an appointment down in your book it carries weight. You can say to people, "Gee, I'm sorry, but I've got that eight-thirty thing and I just can't make it."

♦ **Time-finding Tip #3** ♦

Find time by writing down appointments with yourself in your date book—then no one can take it away from you. When it's in your book in black and white, it's sacred time and you keep it unless it's a life-or-death emergency.

Carol. *"I went for the big one. It's not that I'm so special or that things were so easy for me. But trying to take a little time here and a little time there for myself just wasn't working. And the thing about working is that I've worked since I was in high school. So I decided, that's it, and I just gave myself a sabbatical. I had some money saved up, and I just quit my job. I told everyone, 'I'm taking off work for a year. I need this time for me.' It wasn't like I had this impressive plan in mind. You know, for me it would've been a gift if for a year I just did nothing. Well, I sort of did nothing, but I also had a lot of time to think for the first time in my life, and I came up with a whole new direction for the rest of my life that I hadn't planned on."*

Sometimes you can get a paid sabbatical (although not very often). Sometimes you can take one, but it's unpaid. Sometimes you have to quit your job. But check it out. In an informal survey I did, one out of five women who said they couldn't take a one-year sabbatical found they actually could do this once they really checked it out. You just have to gulp down your fear at taking such a giant step and deal with your sense that you're not entitled to do this.

I think you and I are entitled to do this once a decade. That's how much we are running on empty, running without maintaining connection with why we're doing what we're doing. Taking one year in ten to reenergize and redirect yourself is an incredibly smart investment.

♦ Time-finding Tip #4 ♦

You'll be able to find the time you need if you feel entitled to take the time you need. If you're entitled to take one year in ten for yourself, you are 100 percent entitled to take one year during your life that's completely for you. Entitled? Why I'd order you to do it, if I could.

Donna. *"Einstein said E = mc² — which was saying that matter and energy are the same. Well, in the world of people, time and money are the same. If you've got money, you can always convert it to time, but you* *have to be willing to spend it. That's how I gave myself the gift of a year, and maybe I'm kidding myself, but I think it was the only way I could do it. I hired cleaning people to come in. I ate take-out dinner every day. I redid my budget at work so that it included more support for me, like clerical support, things like that. I went crazy hiring babysitters. I think that year cost me five thousand dollars out of pocket to buy myself that extra time. It was the best money I ever spent."*

I almost didn't include this idea, because I know how many women don't have the money to buy any time for themselves. But this is such a good idea for so many women that I just had to include it. The concept is simplicity itself. You need two, five, ten hours a week for yourself to get the gift of a year? Maybe you can swing it if you hire people to pick up the slack.

♦ Time-finding Tip #5 ♦

Use money to buy time by using money to get people to do things for you that will save you time. The gift of a year is the gift of a lifetime. Don't get hung up on the expense. Don't be afraid to do what you need to do to make it happen. Whatever it costs you, spread out over a lifetime it isn't that much.

Marie. *"You know, I'd actually studied the guitar. But for the last ten years it was just sitting there in the corner like a fat midget lady with a long thin neck and a tiny head, with her hands on her hips mad at me because I was ignoring her. But the longer I went without picking up the guitar, the worse I played when I did pick it up, so it was a kind of vicious circle. I was so excited about the idea of the gift of a year. I thought it was so simple—an hour a day minimum and I figured that twelve months later I'd have my chops back. But I kept not having enough time. Then I looked at where my time went, and I realized there were two women— my mom and my friend Amy who's really my third best friend but she thinks she's my best friend—who were using up practically hours every day on the phone complaining about nothing. I just cut Amy off, and I had to work things out with my mom, not that we didn't have a huge fight* *about it. Once I sort of dealt with Amy and my mom, I had enough time to be a guitar-playing fool."*

Whether at work or in your personal life, there is someone, or maybe two people, who is wasting an amazing amount of your time. Out of all the people in your life, work life and social life combined, 10 percent of them are taking up 90 percent of your time. We all have human time-wasters in our lives. Maybe you feel this is cruel, but you can't say *yes* to yourself until you say *no* to the people who won't let you have a self. They're not sucking you dry deliberately. But they are sucking you dry, and you're letting them.

It's a question of putting up boundaries. When they call, don't stay on the phone. If you know they're calling you, don't take the call. Use your answering machine. Say *no* when they ask you to do things. If someone can neither understand nor respect your need to have time for yourself, maybe this is not the kind of person you want to be taking up much space in your life anyway.

♦ Time-finding Tip #6 ♦

Spend less time with the people who waste the most of your time. Identify the two people in your life who are the two biggest human time-wasters and do whatever you have to do to stop them. Just ask yourself: Do you get anything out of the time you waste with these people?

Connie. *"I don't know about you, but my life is totally filled with all these different things I do. It's not just that my job as an office manager has all these little bits and pieces. But—is everyone's life this complicated?—I don't know, I have all these commitments. So here's what I did. I made a list of the seven . . . I don't know, things in my life that take up the most of my time. My top seven time-taker-uppers. Now check this out. I eliminated the bottom two. I just said I ain't gonna do them anymore. And that's how I had enough time to give myself the gift of a year. It made a new woman out of me."*

Anybody can do this who's looking for time. The one thing that takes up the most time you probably can't do much about—it is probably too important. Little things that barely take up any time, there's not much bang for the buck there. But that intermediate level of things that take up a lot of time but probably aren't so important is fertile ground for making big cuts that will give you big chunks of time.

Every time management book says this—because it's true: you've got to stop spending time on anything but top priority matters. For example, do things you know will help your career a lot, of course, but stop doing things that might help it or only help it a little. Don't do something just because it's urgent if it's also not important. Examine your assignments at work to see if you can't hand one off or even just stop doing it.

Perfectionism is a time-waster—20 percent of the effort you put into any project accomplishes 80 percent of the outcome—so this is a time to ask yourself when good enough is enough and then stop. For everything you do, examine the effort-to-reward ratio—stop doing things when you get to the point where efforts really don't pay off in terms of greater rewards.

You'd be amazed where you can find time. There's TV to cut out, or socializing, or housework you've been doing to impress people you don't care about. There are the weekends. We get so tired that we rationalize just hanging around. But if there's something you're wanting to do with your gift of a year, maybe you can do all your running around *and* all your hanging around on Saturdays and have Sundays for what's really special to you.

Time is like everything else. You find it when you look for it.

There are your lunch hours. Who says you can't take *more* time for lunch and spend *less* time eating to give yourself time for you? It's amazing how many women use their lunch hours to exercise or do other things that are important to them. And you don't have to use your lunch hour for whatever it is that's your gift of a year. You can use it to get things done to free up time for yourself later in the day if that's when you really need the time.

◆ Time-finding Tip #7 ◆

*Take an ax to the activities in your life that drain your time
and aren't that important.* An extra clean house? Extra
special dinners? More TV? More shopping? Imagine
yourself on your deathbed—if you're not going to be
wishing you'd spent more time with these things then,
why do them now?

Lily. *"I always felt my special year was a little lame, because I knew a
lot of women were doing amazing things, but I just wanted to read. I
wanted to get back into reading, not just to stop feeling so ignorant but to
maybe get in touch with something I might be really interested in. But I
needed more time. I'm so proud of myself. It was so simple. I just said no to
everyone, as much as I could, and even when I was afraid I couldn't. Ask
me to do something? Like help you with something at work or go shopping
with you or something? Sorry, but no. I simply said, 'I have an appointment' or 'I'm too tired' or 'I said I would help someone else' or whatever I
thought would get me off the hook. But the thing I told myself was when you
say no, don't let go of your no. Be polite, but keep saying no."*

It couldn't be simpler. Where does our time go? It vanishes every
time we say *yes* to someone. You might not see the effect immediately. But just say *no* to demands on your time for one month, and
the following month you'll feel you've been let out of jail.

◆ Time-finding Tip #8 ◆

Say no whenever and to whomever you can. There is a secret to saying no. First, act very sorry. Second, talk
about having appointments and commitments, but
don't get specific. Third, once you say no, don't let
yourself get talked out of it. Fourth, if they really twist
your arm, tell people it's really hard for you to say *no*
but that this is one time when you just have to.

Lynn. *"You're going to think I'm stupid when I tell you how long it took me to figure this out. But I really wanted to get up early. I just needed time for me. But I was afraid of being tired. That's when it hit me. Oh, yeah, you can get up early and you can go to bed early. Early to bed, early to rise. I was spending time in the evening watching TV, and the thing was I really was too tired to do anything else. It took me awhile to get the rhythm of it to work out, but just having an hour to myself in the morning when everything was quiet and I was well rested was fantastic."*

You have to be careful with this. Most of us are tired already. Cutting back on sleep can be dangerous. But for many women it's possible to rearrange the beginnings and ends of their days to gain one or even two entire hours a day and that may be all you need.

♦ Time-finding Tip #9 ♦

Look for the free time that's already sitting there waiting for you. An extra hour first thing in the morning or an extra hour last thing at night can be the freest, quietest, most liberating time of the day. This can be the time that's easiest to get and best to use.

Lori. *"Here's some help for desperate women. I remember when I said, 'I have no time.' I was convinced. But I was dieting, and my nutritionist had me keep a food diary. And it occurred to me that I should keep a diary of where I was spending my time. Why say I don't have any time before I see where it's really going? I actually bought a second appointment book where I wrote down everything I did with my time. It was a big pain in the neck. But I found a lot of free time."*

The ultimate proof, and the ultimate time-finder, lies in this tip. When you absolutely, positively are sure you have no time, you just have check to see if that's true. And it won't be true. Every woman who says she doesn't eat one extra unnecessary calorie finds she's wrong when she actually keeps track of everything she puts in her mouth. Every woman who says she never spends an unnecessary dollar finds she's wrong when she monitors her expenditures. So get real with yourself when it comes to how you spend your time.

♦ **Time-finding Tip #10** ♦

Find time by keeping track of what you actually do with your time so you can discover where to get more time. In an appointment book you write down what you're going to do when. To find more time, keep a reverse appointment book in which you write down all the things you have done every day just after you do them. No one, when she sees where her time has actually gone, can't find at least three good ways to get more time by eliminating three time-wasters.

Would you be willing to run inside a burning building to save your baby? Of course you would. That's because nothing, absolutely nothing, would be more important than saving your baby's life. That's how we protect our babies—we make them an absolute top priority. Well, it's the same kind of thing when it comes to finding time to give yourself the gift of a year.

The bottom line is absolutely simple. The women who find the time, somehow, are women who make themselves a top priority in their own lives, if only for one year. That's the key behind all the ideas you've just read and whatever great ideas you might come up with yourself. How much time do you think it's worth to save yourself from suffocating?

23

The First Day

*"I think I understand everything,
but how exactly do I start?"*

ou've successfully completed quite a journey. You've thought about what you need and want and considered a whole range of possibilities, and now you have a sense of how you want to spend your special year. You feel entitled, energized, and enthusiastic about giving yourself this gift. And you've come up with some good ideas for how you're going to fit your year into your life and make it work.

You're all set. Congratulations! You have everything you need to make your year a success. Once you see what you want, the gift of a year should be as easy as pie. Follow your heart.

You are all set, but at this point, though, some women don't feel all set yet. If that's you, you want to go, you're ready to go, but something is making it hard for you to go. There's something about taking that first step that's daunting for some women.

Just Do It

Maybe what you need to hear is this: *Just do it.* Yeah, you still have some questions. Yeah, you don't know exactly, precisely down to the last detail what you're going to do. Yeah, you haven't completely figured out how you're going to do it. So you sigh. If only every single one of your ducks was all lined up, then you could go.

Did you ever try to line up ducks? They line themselves up, sometimes. But only if they want to. Only if they're ready. Even if ducks were your profession, you'd be in big trouble if you couldn't do anything until you'd gotten them all lined up.

So, if you'll permit me, and I mean this in the gentlest, most caring way, I hope you'll permit me to give you a kick in the pants. Whatever you're needing before you feel you can get started will only come to you after you get started. That's the *wisdom* behind saying *just do it.*

The Launching Pad

For some women the obstacle to getting started lies in that first day. If you're like this, you feel you're ready to go, but there's something about Day One that's holding you back. What do you do on Day One?

I take this question very seriously. There's a real issue here. Do you remember back in school when you had to write a paper in English class? Sometimes the teacher would give you a topic. Sometimes she'd tell you that you could write about whatever you wanted to write about. Lots of us hated those "whatever you want" assignments. We felt much more comfortable being given a topic. We liked being launched. We weren't quite so comfortable having to do the launching on our own.

There's just something about making the first move that's hard for some women.

So what do you do on Day One? I think the best answer is, "Do as little as possible." I'm talking about something like just sitting quietly for five minutes. That's exactly how I started. The first day of my special year, I just sat there for about five minutes and said, "All right, now. You don't have to take care of anyone. You don't have to do anything. You have a backlog of things you've wanted to do for yourself. You can just start listing them, feeling comfortable with what they are, with knowing what they are."

The point is to take the pressure off. No matter how ambitious you want to be with your special year, there's nothing wrong with letting your first day be a five-minute contemplation of the pleasures ahead of you.

Then what? Don't think of yourself as taking the next step. Instead, think of yourself as seeing the next step to take. You'll take it when you see it. To see the next step to take, here are some questions to ask yourself that will reveal your next step to you.

◆ "What's *one thing* I can do to get started?"

I'll tell you this. If you wait for the perfect thing to do to get started, you'll never get started. The solution is to pick up the first thing in front of you, the first thing that comes to mind, and just go with it. If you don't know what to do to get started, anything you do that makes any sense at all with be just fine.

Here's what a lot of novelists do. They have a sense of their story, just the way you have a sense of your special year. Then they just start, perhaps badly. But they know that once they get going they'll want to change their beginning anyway, so why fuss with it now and keep postponing the launch? Novelists who don't know what they're doing spend a lot of time stuck fiddling with a beginning that they'll never end up using.

It's the same with starting your special year. Momentum is your friend. Perfection is your enemy. Anything you do that gets you going will ultimately work out for you.

◆ "What do I need?"

If you're having the slightest trouble getting started, it may be that there's one crucial missing ingredient, and you can't get going because you haven't really admitted to yourself what it is you need. For example, the way Jennifer, of the bubble baths, tells her story, it sounds as though she just fell into her special year. Well, almost. Actually, Jennifer had a crappy old answering machine. And without realizing it, she was reluctant to take a bath if she had to trust that machine to take her messages. What was the point of a nice relaxing bath if she had to bring the phone with her and take every call?

When she realized that what she needed to get started was a brand new answering machine, Jennifer's logjam was broken.

So ask yourself what the one thing is that you need to feel ready to go, and you'll be on your way.

◆ "How can I have fun with this?"

Some women make things too serious. It's not just the gift of a year. It's oooohhh, the gift of a year. They like it when it feels serious. Because then it feels important. But the more important it feels, the more paralyzed they get. They need to feel it's a big deal to get moving, but they can't get moving because it's such a big deal.

There's only one way out of this trap, honey. Have fun. Forget the serious side of whatever it is you're doing for your special year. Even if your special year is deadly serious. Just think of something you can start with that will be fun, entertaining, simply enjoyable— and your Day One will start out right.

Beyond Day One

There are some things that work to get almost every woman started with her special year. Of course you have to be the final judge of what you need and what works for you. But all of the following ideas are good.

◆ Tell everyone what you're doing.

Why do we have weddings? Because when everyone's in on it, it feels more exciting, happier, more real. The gift of a year is the same. The more people who know about it, the better you'll feel about it. And these people who know about it will actually feed your momentum, perhaps simply by asking you how it's going.

◆ Sketch out a plan.

You've read a whole chapter on planning. All I want to add here is that you should have a sense of how you're going to fit what you want to get from your year into the actual year ahead of you. As I said before, I'm not talking about a *plan* plan. I'm just talking about anything that gives you a sense that you'll be taken care of. Saying "I'll go running every day" is no plan at all. "I'll eat downtown when I leave work so I'm not hungry when I get home and then I'll go running as soon as I change"—that's a plan. It's just enough detail for you to see how what you want to do is doable.

For example, you might want to take out your appointment book and use it as a major tool in your giving yourself the gift of a year. Use it to find time. Use it to make appointments with yourself. Use it to block out sacred time just for you that no one can violate. This too is a plan.

✦ Start a list of options for yourself.

Within whatever you've chosen as your gift of a year, there are always many possibilities. There is never only one way to do anything. So have a little piece of paper in your drawer where you keep a list of options for yourself. Think of these options as a kind of wish list. Give yourself the goal of putting more things on your wish list than you can possibly get.

Do this even if your special year is something as highly defined as getting ready to climb Mount McKinley. You can still do that with different partners. On different dates. By different routes. You can give yourself more or less time to do the actual climb.

The reason to give yourself a ton of options is to give yourself a few pounds of really good options. The person who said that the way to have a lot of good ideas is to have a lot of ideas and then weed out the bad ones was absolutely correct. This is what geniuses do, and I can tell you from personal experience that it works beautifully for nongeniuses. Create a lot of options, ignore the least good options, and you'll have made your special year 100 percent better.

✦ Write yourself a letter.

As has usually been the case in my work, this idea doesn't come from me telling women what to do, it comes from women telling me what's worked for them. The letter technique is beautiful. And simple. At the very beginning of your special year—this is what you can do on Day One if you want—write a little letter to yourself. It doesn't have to be more than one page. Just write down what your gift of a year is. Write down what you're planning to do. Write down why you're doing it. And write down what you're hoping to get from it.

This is your testament to yourself about the meaning and importance your special year has for you. This is where you bear witness to what you need and why you need it. This is where you create a picture for yourself of the small dream you're trying to achieve.

Women tell me that this letter keeps them focused, optimistic, and on course. Think of it almost as a little map showing you the route from your heart to a piece of happiness that lies in your future.

Beyond all the tips and words of wisdom, the very best suggestion for how to get started with the gift of a year now that you've come this far is just do it,

just do it,

just do it,

just do it,

just do it,

just do it.

BUILDING ON WHAT YOU'VE GOTTEN

24

Loving Our Lives

"How can I look for my special year
to change my life?"

’ve counseled women for twenty-five years. For every single woman I’ve worked with, I’ve felt I was holding her life and her heart in my hands. I can’t imagine doing anything more important.

And for every woman I work with, there always comes the time to say goodbye. This is the moment we look forward to. It’s graduation. And every time just before we say goodbye, I always ask myself if there’s one last thing I need to say, even though our work is done.

Well, here we are, you and I, and this work of ours together is done. And I’ve asked myself if I have one last thing to say to you.

I do. What I want to say to you is: “Don’t forget to let your special year change your life, if that’s at all possible.”

Of course I have no idea how your particular year will change your life. But you don’t either. It’s an adventure. I’m just asking you to remember to be open.

I do know this. In the midst of your jam-packed life you have grabbed hold of a piece of time to give yourself the gift of *you*. You’ve done something special to take care of yourself. Or you’ve done something to fulfill a dream. How can you be the same afterward? How can your life be the same? Whatever change your special year brings you, let it happen. You don't have to force it. Just don't resist it.

Let me reassure you about something, though. Nothing has to rock your world. Nothing big has to change in your life unless you want it to. There's nothing wrong with taking a year for yourself to renew and refresh, or just to add a missing piece to your life. And then you go back to things the way they were, feeling better about yourself and your life. You've had a positive experience that maybe you'll want to have again. What could be simpler than that?

So the pressure's off. I want you to know that. Enjoy yourself.

Unless you want to consider the possibility of opening one more door.

Welcome to Your Secret Garden

You've opened so many doors already by giving yourself the gift of a year. Why not consider opening one more door? It looks modest from the outside. But by opening it you might be able to go places you never imagined.

The door I'd like you to think about opening is the door to changes you can't yet imagine.

You've met a lot of women so far. They've told you their own stories about their own special years. I'd like to share with you some different voices now, the voices of people close to these women telling what they saw and heard and experienced. That's a kind of proof, isn't it, that something's really changed you? When it's visible from the outside.

These little vignettes are offered to inspire you. I hope that if you catch a taste of a few ways the gift of a year changed some women's lives, some unique possibility that's yours alone will reveal itself to you. There's only one thing I want you to take from these stories. *Dare to dream.* You'll never know what's in your secret garden until you open yourself up to the possibility of exploring it.

My sister Claudia. "It always makes you sad when someone close to you is sad. That's how I'd always felt about my kid sister Claudia. She was okay and everything, but she'd been so bubbly as a little girl, and as a woman she seemed to have this permanent case of the blues, the blahs . . . she was just always a little down. Like soda that was left out and went flat. Like her life was going through the motions, and she didn't care. She faked happiness. But it just came across as a kind of brittle perkiness. I knew her, and there was something missing.

"Then she gave herself the gift of a year. When I first heard about it I thought it was about Claudia just taking a bit of a rest because she worked hard, and I knew she needed that. But she was never busier in her life than during her special year.

"I don't know where she got this idea from. She told me it was something she'd been thinking about doing for a long time. Anyway, Claudia immediately got going with this intensive program where you learn to teach English as a second language. She lived in a West Coast city where they have a lot of immigrants. A lot of them refugees. I guess she'd known a lot of people like that who'd been here for a long time and were very lost.

"Within that year Claudia's blah blues left her. She was like a teacher, hostess, mother all at the same time. She'd been some kind of analyst for a securities firm. That must've seemed very empty to her, although the money was good. Now she was both saving people's lives and becoming part of their communities. She had to be happy to do her new job well, but it made her so happy to do her new job well. The gift of a year gave me back the sister I'd grown up with. She followed up on a dream, got a new career, and found the missing key to happiness for her."

My best friend Irene. "Let me tell you right off that Irene was always the warmest, most giving, most loving person I knew. If you were her friend she'd chop her arm off if that would help you. It made her happy to be that way. So all that was great. But here's the fly in the ointment. She was loyal, obviously. But she was married to this . . . well, he was way beyond being a dud. He was a slob, a slug, an oaf. Irene would chop her arm off for you. But if Irene had a heart attack this guy would just sit there. It's not just me. All of her friends and her mother kept saying she should leave him. Her daughter said mommy I don't know why you stay with daddy.

"But here was the thing. Irene didn't feel very good about herself. I knew she'd had a lot of problems in school. I guess they misdiagnosed her dyslexia and thought she was stupid. So Irene thought she deserved a guy like her husband. Plus she was grateful to him for I don't know what. Just being there, I guess, with her who thought she had nothing to offer.

"That was the situation. Then she decided to give herself this gift of a year. I think when she started all she knew was that she wanted to find a way to turn something around in her life somewhere. Because she'd also been a bartender for a long time, and she was very good at it. But she didn't respect it. Not as something she kept doing year after year. She didn't want her kids to go to high school and have to say that their mother was a bartender.

"So after Irene started her year she got the idea of starting a restaurant. It's a long story, but there was the possibility of doing something with the place next to the bar where she worked. And they could link up. It was sort of complicated. Irene needed to learn things about business, she needed to line up financing, which meant talking to some rich guys she knew from the bar—and she needed to line up suppliers. It was a whole megillah. But what Irene had was dogged persistence. So I guess for one year Irene spent a little less time hanging out with us, God bless her, and put together a little business.

"Now, you see, I don't care about the business part. I'm glad for her, but the big deal was that once she got the business started she realized that she didn't have to be grateful to this bum of a guy who tied himself to her and made her miserable. What Irene got was freedom from guilt. That's the big backdoor benefit Irene got from the gift of a year."

My wife Pam. "I don't know if there's anything worse than loving someone and watching their life spin out of control. On the surface I guess Pam was an achiever, but we were all afraid it was going to blow up. She was an associate at a really nice downtown law firm.

Supposedly she specialized in environmental law. The thing was that she had a really good chance of making partner. The firm needed a woman partner, and for a variety of reasons they wanted a presence in environmental law.

"But Pam had this way of running around like a nut. She would join committees. She'd take on all kinds of extra little assignments at work she didn't have to and that she knew wouldn't help her make partner. She had this idea of writing a book about an environmental agenda for the twenty-first century. All good stuff. And our house had to be a showplace.

"She spread herself paper thin. Vapor thin. There was none of her to go around. Nothing got done right, and she was exhausted. Then she heard from someone who heard from someone that they were having questions about her at the law firm. I don't know how she heard about the gift of a year, but I was terrified because I was afraid that she would just put something else on her plate. But it was great. Pam suddenly radically simplified everything. Instead of being Wonder Woman and trying to please everyone and save everyone, she said she would just take care of herself. She'd have one priority, she said. And that was to get what she wanted. And what she wanted was to make partner because then she'd start to have some real power to do what she cared about in her life.

"The gift of a year for Pam was just not doing anything except those things at the firm that would shine a beacon on her partner potential. Just do important work and win. It was painful for her to let stuff go. But I could see how exciting it was to feel she was focusing on what really mattered to her and what might have some kind of payoff. She said to me, 'You know, for me the gift of a year is proving I can focus.'

"Okay, Pam made partner. But we'd always thought she would before she started going nuts with her commitments. The big change was like an inner glow, a calm, almost an inner Zen thing where Pam was centered and strong and confident. And I'm telling you, it wasn't because of her success. It was because she gave herself a gift where she learned to relax and have focus and let go. Pam became everything she'd always been, but better. Brought to a kind of ripeness."

*   *   *

Three stories. Three lives. Out of countless other instances where the gift of a year had some long-lasting benefit because of some way it changed a woman's life. Don't take these stories as your road map. What you should take from these stories is the idea that anything is possible once you take the time to give yourself what you need. Just be open to everything that's possible for you as your special year unfolds.